Memoirs
~ of ~
Dennison Leslie Bruno

Pilot Officer
RCAF

Chief Master Sergeant
USAF, Retired

Ex-POW / Stalag IV B

Published by
Dennison Leslie Bruno
Abilene, TX 79602

To my wife, Ruby, whose love
and support made this book possible.

Dennison Leslie Bruno
Pilot Officer, RCAF
1945

Chapter 1

Where to begin? The best place is probably with my mother Margaret, or Maggie, as she was generally known. I can't recall many calling her Margaret. She was born in the hill country around Turriff in northeast Scotland in 1889. Her mother had ten children fathered by two husbands. Poverty and hard work was the normal expectation for the vast majority of Scottish families, especially in the rural areas, and her family was no exception. However one way to break the cycle of poverty was to immigrate to some other country, preferably somewhere in the British Empire. Since the fare to Canada was one of the cheaper tickets, it was one of the most popular. How she saved enough for her passage I do not know. Perhaps she received some help from a number of family members, some of whom had already made it to Canada. Maggie arrived in Canada just before the outbreak of World War One, which quickly became an era of full employment. Before long Maggie had a job in a munitions factory. The wages were higher in order to compensate for the danger. The factory and Maggie survived the war years without serious incident. Near the end of the war she met her husband to be, Sergeant Joe Bruno. He was an American by birth from Lawrence, Massachusetts. His mother's maiden name was Kelly who came from County Cork in Ireland and his father was mainly of Italian extraction. At age fifteen he managed to join the American Navy by concealing his true age, but was later booted out. Still searching for adventure he went to Canada to enlist in the Army. Canada had followed Britain into the war, while the United States was still attempting to stay neutral.

His unit, the 4th Battalion was an infantry unit, which had been recruited in the Toronto area. As soon as training was completed the 4th Battalion was on its way to France. Joe managed to survive a couple of years in the trenches. Most of the time he was assigned to a heavy machine-gun. His luck finally ran out during a fierce German counter-attack on their portion of the front. In the hand-to-hand fighting he was shot and bayoneted in the face. He continued to fight on, killing several Germans. He then picked up the captain of his unit who had been badly wounded and managed to carry him back to a First Aid station. This engagement resulted in his receiving a Distinguished Conduct Medal and his wounds caused him to be shipped home to Canada. The jagged scar across the left side of his face was another decoration he would carry the rest of his life.

I am not aware of how my parents met, but they were married soon after his return from France. One of his first jobs was a steeplejack, but this did not last long. He liked to drink and loved to gamble and never could stick with any job for very long. In 1918 their first baby, a girl, was born. They named her Myrtle. Another girl Agnes followed in 1921, but the marriage was very rocky. Joe was just not a good provider. Sometimes he was gone for days, only to reappear either flat broke or with a wad of money, depending on how the cards had fallen. The old cliché about opposites attracting was very evident in this marriage. Maggie never touched a drop of liquor or smoked. Joe enjoyed both. Maggie was thrifty and saving like most Scots. Joe had an easy come, easy go style. Maggie was raised Presbyterian and attended church irregularly. Joe was Catholic and in a lax sort of way. Finally, when their third child a boy was born in 1923, Maggie decided on a separation. She chose my name Dennison from a book she was reading at the time of my birth. A few months later Maggie moved out taking the children with her. Working all day and taking care of three children was a real struggle.

There was a Catholic-run day care center called the Crèche which helped working mothers by caring for their children. However Maggie was reluctant to have her children raised Catholic so looked for other answers to her problem of childcare. I was the big problem being so young at that time. This part I don't remember, but my mother told about me getting up at the crack of dawn, getting out my window, and she would have to find me when she got up. At that time we lived about a half mile from a park that had a carrousel which I loved and I often ended up there. One morning she looked out and the milkman's horse and wagon were standing in our street and I was running around under the horse's legs.

When the girls, Agnes and Myrtle, reached school age, Maggie arranged for me to go live with her aunt and uncle. Aunt Nellie and Uncle Archie had a small farm near Agincourt, a town about forty-five miles north of Toronto. Nellie and Archie Leslie was a childless couple in their early fifties at that time. The farm was probably less than a hundred acres, with a good orchard, vegetable garden, chickens, and a herd of about twenty-five beef and dairy cattle. I was about four years old when I went to live there. Even so, I can remember some things that happened.

I remember Prince their mixed breed collie. Aunt Nellie sometimes gave me a pot to clean out when she had finished cooking something. Prince and I would share this from the same spoon. There was a calf named Fairy which I used to try and ride like a horse. I remember in the cellar there were always a couple of barrels set up on stands that were filled with apple juice in the fall. These changed to cider and I think eventually vinegar. The barrels had spigots on them and I guess I enjoyed getting a drink from those barrels regardless of what fermentation stage they were going through.

There were also some less pleasant memories. Anything put on my plate I was required to eat or sit there until I did. I had a real problem with fatty meat and would gag trying to force it down. The old adage "Spare the rod and spoil the child," was firmly enforced in that household.

A calf named, Fairy. She did not want me
riding her like a bucking bronco. (1926)

My buddy, Prince. (1926)

Chapter 2

One incident that I remember vividly occurred after I had been there for some time. On the north boundary of the farm was a county road with wide banks on each side, usually covered with lush grass and wildflowers during the growing season. Uncle Archie would sometimes take the cattle out there to graze. Someone would have to stay with the herd to prevent them going up on to the railway which ran on the west boundary of the farm. At five years old, I sometimes had this task of keeping the cattle from straying past the level crossing or on to the railway. This was often boring and lonely for me as a five year old. However you could get a real good close up view of any train that happened to come by. On this particular day, I was standing at the level crossing, patiently waiting and hoping for a train to come along. I could see some smoke in the distance from the station in Agincourt. The level crossing was covered with wooden boarding and I had unconsciously wriggled one foot down between one of the rails and a board while eagerly watching the train as it started coming up the line. The train was now picking up speed and rapidly approaching so I started to move back, away from the tracks. It was then I discovered my foot was jammed. Panicked and frightened, I was frantically trying to pull free while all the time the train was getting closer. I had skinned my ankle trying to get free but the shoe would not budge. The engineer was steadily blowing the whistle. Whether he was blowing it for the level crossing or whether he could actually see me I did not know. About that time my Guardian Angel went to work and my foot came out of my shoe. I knew I would be in trouble if I went home with a mangled shoe, so I reached down and managed to jerk it free before scampering off the tracks. The train thundered past while I stood there shaken, but relieved. I was afraid to tell Aunt Nellie or Uncle Archie what had happened but I had nightmares about trains for quite a while.

On another occasion, I attempted to stop a very persistent cow from getting up to the railway track, but I or the small stick that I was using to block her way did not impress this particular cow. She bunted me in the face, sending me reeling back with a nosebleed. So much for the trials and tribulations of a young cowhand.

I suppose I was lonely a lot of the time while living with Archie and Nellie. They were a hard humorless couple but I enjoyed being around all the animals on the farm. My mother would come for a visit about one Sunday a month. These visits were often traumatic for me and probably for her also. I would often cry and beseech her to take me with her. Sundays were sort of special for another reason because we went to the Presbyterian Church in Agincourt. In Sunday school, we children were taught to sing some hymn, which we would then get to sing to the church congregation. I remember we would belt out "Jesus wants me for a sunbeam" with great gusto.

I started to attend school in Agincourt, either kindergarten or first grade; I'm not sure which grade it was. My main memory of this was that I was left handed, but any time I dared to touch a pencil with my left, hand I was whacked across the knuckles with a ruler. I had a tricycle with a very large front wheel, which I rode to school, as there was no school bus service in those days. An occasional visitor at Agincourt was my mother's oldest brother Uncle Alec. His visits always seem to end up with him and Archie getting very drunk. The one visit I remember the most, started with them drinking while they waited for someone else who was supposed to be coming. They were both upset about something this guy had done and after a lot of drinks decided he deserved hanging for his crime. Out to the barn they went and fashioned a noose and hung the rope over one of the rafters. Then they return to the kitchen and few more drinks while they wait for the guilty party to arrive. Aunt Nellie, who was thoroughly alarmed at all this, quietly instructed me to go out to the barn and hide the rope. Fortunately nobody else came that night and everyone went to sleep.

My departure from Agincourt was a surprise to me and very abrupt. My mother came on a visit and discovered a lot of black and blue marks on me. We left the same day.

Chapter 3

That summer of 1929, I was sent to live with a minister and his family. I believe they lived somewhere near the town of Port Hope, about sixty miles east of Toronto. There were three or four children in the family, all of whom were older than I. Of course Sunday was the big day in this family, but I do not remember those days with a lot of pleasure. We attended two church services and Sunday school and no playtime was allowed on Sunday. Grace was said at every meal and was so lengthy; meals were usually cold by the time we got to eat. There was a small organ in the parlor on which the minister's wife often played hymns during the evenings or on Sunday afternoon. I was not mistreated but my memory of living with this family was of a very dull existence. As a child I could not understand why I was separated from my family. Only a child that has endured that kind of separation can understand the loneliness and hurt. But a new chapter of my life was about to begin.

One of Maggie's sisters, Georgina Connon, who still lived in Scotland, was aware of the struggle that Maggie was having, to make a living and raise a family. Georgina was a widow with three children of her own. Her husband Dodd Connon had gone to Canada to get established and the family was to follow as soon as money for fares could be saved. On a sad day in Toronto he was running to catch a streetcar when he tripped and fell under the wheels of the lorry and died that same night. Georgina and her children, Willie, Bobby and Margaret, were left in poor circumstances. However good fortune suddenly smiled on Georgina with the offer of a position to take care of a rather large estate for a family named Turner. The Turner family did not live on this particular estate called Turner Hall; it was nevertheless an imposing place, with several hundred acres of property. The Turners used the estate occasionally for bird hunting, and also for wonderful fruits and vegetables grown in a very large garden.

Aunt Georgina now wrote to my mother, suggesting I be sent to live with her for a while, since her new position provided her with a nice house and a great place to raise children. This sounded wonderful to my mother, compared to trying to raise me in the big city of Toronto as a single parent. Arrangements were made for me to leave in September 1929.

When the day came for me to leave, my mother took me to Union Station in Toronto. With a small trunk for my clothes and a note pinned to my lapel I boarded the train for Montreal. The parting was probably much harder for my mother than it was for me, as I had no conception of the time or distance I would be traveling. In Montreal, I was met by someone from the Cunard White Star Steamship Line, and taken to the docks to board the Steamship Latisha, one of the older ships on the Trans Atlantic run. I remember being upset because I was separated from my trunk in customs; however it miraculously turned up in my cabin when I went on board.

It did not take long for most of the passengers and crew to know I was traveling alone, so
a lot of them took an interest in my welfare. An elderly gentleman tried to teach me to play chess. My dinner companions would help me with the menus. I remember ordering a dish of olives thinking they were some kind of fruit. People tried to get me to order something different but I was adamant. When I bit into the first olive I was shocked at the sour taste. I think everyone was waiting to see my reaction, so I pretended to like them and forced myself to eat the whole dish. I pretty well had the run of the ship. In the main salon in the evenings they had a horse racing game where different little wooden horses were advanced around a track by the roll of the dice. I was not allowed to play but did get to shake the dice in a cup and roll the numbers. The winners would often tip me, so I ended the voyage with more money than I started.

The North Atlantic gets its share of storms in the fall and winter months and on about the third day we ran into a good one. I remember going on deck to find that ropes had been strung to keep people back from the rails and to provide something to hang on to as the ship rose and fell in the giant rollers. It was exciting to watch the waves coming as they appeared higher than the ship but at the last moment the ship would rear up and only a heavy spray would hit the decks. A lot of the passengers were seasick, but I enjoyed the whole thing. It took about a week to reach Glasgow, Scotland where two ladies who were friends of Aunt Georgina met me, and put on the train to Aberdeen. In Aberdeen Aunt Georgina met me. This wonderful woman would be a substitute mother for me for some of the happiest years of my childhood.

Aunt Georgina
She treated me like part of the family. (1967)

Chapter 4

A few days later we moved to Turner Hall about three miles from the town of Ellen, where we children would attend school. At the entrance to the estate was a stone cottage for the gatekeeper. Since no gatekeeper lived there it was overgrown with ivy and other shrubbery. From there the main driveway was lined with beautiful hardwood trees, rhododendron and lilac bushes and a strange variety of trees with a thorny trunk we call "Monkey Puzzle Trees." I'm not sure if that is the proper name for them but that is what we called them. A small road led off to the left to the Gardener's cottage and a ten acre walled garden. Boxwood hedges lined the planting beds and stone crushed walkways throughout the garden. Jimmy Ellis, the gardener, his wife Aggie, who was also a great aunt to me, and the Connons had three children. The boys were named Jimmy and Sydney and the youngest Evie, was a girl. Evie was retarded, and did not attend school. Jimmy Ellis also had his mother living with them. She was crazy and would sometimes run off. We kids would have to hunt for her and pull and push her back home. Jimmie was a little strange also but he knew how to take care of a garden. What fruits and vegetables the Turner family did not take was available for the Connons and the Ellis family to use. Both families always ate well.

The driveway continued on up to the main house. This was a big Victorian era three level mansion with an added glassed observation room or tower. From here on a clear day you could se the North Sea coastline, about seventeen miles away. The house had about sixteen bedrooms. In the scullery next to the kitchen was a long row of bells, which connected to velvet pull ropes in various rooms as a means to summon servants. There was a wine cellar sans wine, and one locked room, which probably contained some of the more expensive items left at the estate. The house was fully furnished with beautiful eighteenth century pieces, including three pianos and one organ. White dust covers draped most of the furniture.

We children had the run of the whole estate. Wooded sections contained an assortment of hard woods. Some sections were pine planted in neat rows about six feet apart. Branches from one tree meshed with those next to them. We could climb these trees and move from tree to tree like a bunch of apes. Between tree groupings were several small fenced pastures. In one of these was a pigeon house. The interior walls were honey combed with slate boxes for nesting. The house that was provided for Aunt Georgina and family was situated close to a large carriage house, which still contained a few carriages. Nearby were large room-sized cages for hunting dogs. I don't know what kind of dogs they kept or what they hunted. The only wild game we had was rabbits and hares. In the bird department were pidgins and grouse.

The men in the Turner family and their friends would usually come about once a year to do some grouse shooting. We kids would be hired for the day to act as 'beaters' to make the birds fly, for which we were paid five shillings each. Living on an estate with five shillings in your pocket! Who could ask for anything more? Starting school in Ellen was a little tough at first. I was the strange kid with a strange name that nobody had ever heard of, and besides that I talked funny. Different grades got out of school at different times so with no cousins around I had to fight my way out of the school yard. Fortunately they quickly tired of this sport and left me alone. I liked going to school. The worst thing was the three-mile walk to get there and three more coming home in all kinds of weather.

Chapter 5

The following year my aunt Georgina decided to raise a flock of turkeys to sell before the Christmas season. Everything went well and the turkeys were sold off early in December. She kept one large one we named Tom for our Christmas dinner. Since he was now alone, Tom followed us kids around and became a kind of pet. Come time to kill him, we kids were reluctant to do so, but Aunt Georgina insisted it had to be done. With a poker from the fireplace, we put it across his neck, held each end down with our feet and pulled his neck thinking he was dead, we dropped him but he scrambled to his feet and ran off. Next time it worked. At Christmas, none of us wanted to eat any turkey.

One summer a butcher in the town of Ellen rented one of the meadow fields for a small herd of horses he owned. We would corner one of the smaller sizes and one person would run in and grab the mane and jump on. Everyone scattered as the horse ran to rejoin the rest of the herd bucking as it went, so you were back on the ground pretty quick. One day when we went to the meadow we found that one of the horses had died. We went into town to tell the butcher about it. He said he would give us one pound to dig a hole to bury the horse. We agreed to do so not realizing how big a hole you had to dig to bury a horse. I think it took us two days.

Our grandparents lived about forty miles away at a place called "The Binn" three miles north of the town of Huntly. At the time of my first visit my great grandmother was living there, but died shortly thereafter. Three unmarried uncles still lived at home; Archie, Willie and Douglas. Archie worked in a grocery store in Huntly, the rest of the men did forestry work, felling trees, stripping branches and bark. On weekends they had a family band. My grandmother played piano, Willie played the fiddle, Archie the saxophone and Douglas on drums. Occasionally they would play for local dances but mostly for their own enjoyment. My grandmother's death ended the band's existence.

We had lived at Turner Hall for two years when we were told the sad news. The Turner family could no longer afford the taxes they had to pay so they planned on selling the contents of Turner Hall and level the house. The contents of the main house were sold at auction. Rolls Royce and Bentley automobiles lined the driveway around the house. We moved before the demolition of the house. We moved to the Binn so that aunt Georgina could keep house for my grandfather and my uncles. I attended the Gordon School in Huntly. After a year my aunt tired of keeping house for so many men so we moved again to a house on a farm in Conniecluch about three miles from Huntly as the crow flies but seven miles by road. So walking to school was across fields through an area we called The Craw Woods because hundreds of crows roosted there every night. Their raucous chorus when they left in the morning to forage for food and settling down in the evening was deafening. From the woods I would come out on a road that led past the ruins of

Huntly Castle on my way to school. I did not like going pass the castle after dark because it was supposedly haunted by ghosts but I never saw any.

On the way from school one day I found a baby bird that had fallen from the nest. Unable to locate the nest I took the bird home. We dug worms and pushed them down its throat and fed it other bugs we could find. As its feathers grew we realized the bird was a Jackdaw, which looks like a small sized raven. Jackie, as we named him or her, rode around perched on my shoulder. After learning to fly he would sit and wait for me on my way home from school and would dive down and perch on my shoulder. If I started to turn my head in his direction he would peck my ear, so I would not knock him off. After several months he disappeared and we never knew what happened to him.

One day a swarm of bees appeared over our small garden we had outside the house. We started beating on pails and wash drums as the noise was supposed to help them settle. Settle, they did, but under the sloping tile roof of our house and the inside bedroom slanted ceiling upstairs. Several months later on a Saturday when my aunt Georgina had gone to town to shop, we decided to get the honey away from the swarm. We managed to loosen the ceiling panel behind where the swarm was located. We made some smoking torches with damp newspapers to smoke the bees out. It worked pretty well except that some of the bees got into the house. Between bees, smoke, burnt newspapers and a trail of honey from the bedroom to the kitchen we had quite a mess. Then trying to melt the honey out of the combs in a pot over the fire, we ended up with burnt tasted honey. Needless to say Aunt Georgina was pretty upset when she came home.

The farm where we lived was primarily devoted to sheep. I spent one summer with the Shepherd tending the sheep. Summer is a busy time around sheep. They have to be dipped and sheared and the herd thinned to a level the farm could sustain. The rams were pastured separately from the main flock and given special feed. One day I had taken a bag of feed to dump in their feeding trough. Usually I kept a wary eye on them because they would keep their head down and knock you into the middle of next week. This time I was careless and one of them sent me crashing into the fence. Fortunately I had no serious injury. I did have a close call in the stables where the draft horses were kept. These were Belgian's with huge iron-shod feet. One day when I walked behind the open end of their stalls one of the horses suddenly lashed out with two back feet. He missed me but smashed the boards of the wooden walls of the stable. I guess I surprised him and I learned that was the wrong thing to do.

One summer I went to visit my great aunt Agnes and family at their new work location at Stricken House. This is the family that was the gardener at Turner Hall. I spent about a month there. The one thing I remember about Stricken House is that a Druid Circle existing on the estate. Although overgrown with vegetation the circle of stones and the altar were still in place. It always gave us a strange feeling knowing that human sacrifices had probably been made on this spot.

Jackie, sitting on his favorite perch. (1933)

Huntly Castle was sort of spooky after dark. (1934)

Chapter 6

In early 1935 a letter arrived from my mother saying I had to return to Canada or lose my Canadian citizenship. Arrangements were made for me to go by train to Glasgow to board the ship for Montreal. This ship was the Canard White Star liner Athenia. This ship would be the first ship sunk by a German U boat in World War II.

Arriving back in Toronto I had to start my life all over again. I was a stranger in my home, twelve years old. I went to Courcelette Road School. Now I was the 'strange kid with the funny Scotch accent', which I tried to lose in a hurry.

During my first year after returning to Canada my mother decided that I needed to take Hawaiian guitar lessons. I had no talent or interest in learning to play so after a few weeks with little progress my music career ended. That year when cold weather came I learned about ice hockey. Our school janitor always flooded a boarded area of the schoolyard when the weather got cold to provide us kids with a place to play hockey. We played at lunchtime and after school. Since I was just learning how to skate I usually played goalie. With only a couple of magazines stuffed in my socks for protection it was a painful experience. I very quickly learned to skate so I wouldn't have to play goalie anymore.

The following year of school in the seventh grade started out badly for me. At the end of the first semester my grades were terrible. Our teacher always rearranged the class seating so that those students with the lowest grades sat at the front of the class and good students sat in the back. I was ashamed and embarrassed to be one of the ones seated in the front. It must have been a wake-up call for me for by the next report card I made it to the back row and stayed there for the remainder of the year.

In that same year I got a paper route. In those days Toronto had three newspapers. The Globe and Mail was a morning paper and the Toronto Star and Evening Telegram were afternoon additions. The Star and the Telegram were the ones I delivered. The papers were dumped off on Kingston Road about a half-mile from my house. It was best to be there when the papers came between 4 and 4:30 so that in case of rain or snow they wouldn't get wet. I delivered 175 or more papers every day except Sunday. We did have to collect from our customers and then pay for the newspapers. The first thing I did was start saving for a bicycle. It took several months before I could buy one. This made my delivery service, when it wasn't snowing, a lot easier. I delivered papers all through my 7th, 8th, 9th, and 10th grades. Usually I had good relations with the customers and the dogs on my route, except for one 'run in' with a German shepherd. A retired policeman had this shepherd in his back yard with a high wooden fence. I had to go down a lane beside his house to deliver to a house behind him. This German shepherd would leap at the top of the fence as I rode by on my bike going in and coming out, but one day somehow he managed to get over the fence as I was going out of the lane and he charged after me. He caught me before I could get to the street and knocked me off my bicycle. I was under the bike trying to keep the dog from biting me when the owner ran out and pulled the dog off me. I ended up getting a free pair of trousers from the owner of the dog. He added another 2 feet of wire above the fence so that didn't happen again.

Chapter 7

When I was in the 8th grade a new Boy Scout Troop was formed at our school. The Scoutmaster's name was Mr. Rimmer. He was a WWI veteran and an ex-Royal Canadian Mounted Police officer and one of the finest men I have ever known. I became a part of the Beaver Patrol. Our patrol leader was Billy Walton who could have passed for "the Fonz" from the television series "Happy Days". We had lots of fun and learning experiences going camping, swimming, horseback riding. One year we went camping at Shadow lake and I was one of those who went early to help set up camp and stayed late to help take everything down again. There was a riding stable nearby and when you wanted to go riding the owner would take you out to the pasture in an old convertible and he would rope the horses we were going to be riding and bring them back to the stable so we could saddle them.   After several times when I always seemed to get a slow moving horse, I asked the owner for a horse that would run. The next time he roped a big raw-boned ugly horse for me to ride. I quickly found out that this horse was an old lead horse trained to lead the other horses and he could not tolerate any horse being in front of him. Going out from the stable was not a problem, however as soon as we turned for home he would take the bit in his mouth and go at a full gallop. We were coming down a dirt road when a car approached head on and I was desperately trying to pull him off the road. At the last minute he saw the car and leaped on a huge boulder on the side of the road and when the car passed he jumped back on the road and headed on to the stable. He wouldn't stop and I had to duck to get through the doorway - he knew where the oats were kept. The owner was upset because the horse was all lathered up, so I never rode that horse again.

As a teenager the Boy Scouts were a positive influence that provided a set of values that helped me in future years. It did not however prevent a lot of foolish escapades. For example tying ourselves together with rope and trying to cross the face of a sand stone cliff called Scarborough Bluffs on the shore of Lake Ontario. With hand axes we tried to cut hand holds and foot holds. By some miracle we never fell. Another clever trick in the winter when ice formed along the edge of the lake there would always be bobbing chunks of ice floes that had broken off. We would jump from one to another of these ice floes. Sometimes one would start floating away from the shore and we would have to throw a rope to whoever was on it and pull them back in. And then there was the railway bridge over the Rouge River close to where it ran into Lake Ontario. One hot summer day we decided to climb up the steel frame work and see who could hang on to a railroad tie when a train passed overhead. We sat on the rails until we could see a train coming then climbed down and got in position. The train rumbled onto the bridge belching smoke and dropping hot cinders on us. It was too scary and we let go and dropped into the river below. Once was enough so we never tried it again.

One person I grew to admire was George Butcher. George had been stricken with rheumatic fever and was bedridden for two years. He was still trying to keep up with his schooling so our teacher would give his lessons to one of us students to drop off at his home. The Butcher's had a Bull Terrier named "Jake" who only allowed George's mother and doctor to touch his bed. Anybody else got a warning growl.

Mr. Butcher was a German immigrant with German work ethics. He caught the same streetcar every day and would return home at night at almost the same time each work day. Jake must have had his own alarm clock because about a minute before Mr. Butcher was to arrive, Jake would go to the front door to greet him. Mr. Butcher smoked a pipe and sometimes he would give his lighted pipe to Jake to hold in his clenched teeth. I don't think he liked it but he was quite a sight with that smoking pipe in his mouth. George recovered sufficiently so that he that he could attend school again. On the way to school I would stop by and pull him in his little red wagon over to the school. Our whole class looked after George and got him to anywhere he wanted to go. I think he read the entire Encyclopedia Britannica for the two years he was bedridden because he was really smart in school. When the 155th Boy Scout troop was formed George became a scout. By this time he was walking with a severe limp and could ride a bicycle. A memorable bicycle ride occurred when we heard that Group Captain Billy Bishop, a Canadian World War I Flying Ace was coming to Toronto and would land at the Island Airport. This was about a ten mile ride for us but we were there when his plane landed. It was evident he was drunk when he staggered off the plane. We were shocked and disappointed in our hero. George and I worked on earning our King Scout badges together, which is equivalent to America's Eagle Scout badge. Later on when World War II started George would become the Scout Master of the troop while the rest of us went off to war.

In the eighth grade, George, Ray Bradshaw and I sat in the same row behind one another and we would compete for grades. On one particular test we three topped the class with a 99 score which made it look like we had cheated. Fortunately we had each made a different mistake. Ray and I became fast friends. He helped me with my paper route and took over when I could not be there. He owned a canoe so we spent a lot of time on the water of Lake Ontario. About eighteen miles east of Toronto is a place called Frenchman's Bay. The shoreline curved between Toronto and the Bay so it was a much shorter distance to cut across rather than follow the shore. At mid-point this meant that you were about three miles from shore. On Saturday evening we would paddle to Frenchman's Bay, and watch the dancers at an open pavilion and then sleep on the beach that night. We would paddle back on Sunday afternoon providing the weather was still holding. However, sometimes we would leave the canoe with one of the cottagers and hitchhike home on the highway and then go back later when the weather permitted to get the canoe. One of the Assistant Scout Masters, Jim Twining, decided to build a catamaran, a sailboat with one pontoon, which we named the "Swoose." After it was finished, Jim didn't care for it so Ray and I bought it from him. This was much easier than paddling the canoe and a lot more fun. On Saturday nights we would anchor off shore at the Balmy Beach

Canoe Club and listen to the music of the dance band inside.

Another summer outing I always enjoyed was a visit to my Aunt Agnes, my mother's sister. She and her husband Dick and three cousins Betty, Margaret and Billy lived on a farm near Ellesmere an area now swallowed up by Toronto. Uncle Dick managed a farm owned by a mining engineer. The farm was just a hobby with a few riding horses, a couple of milk cows, chickens, ducks, a few hay fields and pastures. Part of the land was wooded with a good size creek running through it. The owner decided to build an earth dam on the creek to provide an area for swimming. A framework of logs was first laid across the creek to anchor the dam. In order to provide rock and dirt for the dam the owner brought in a mining cart and rails to run it on. There was a high bank about seventy five yards from the creek and the plan was to blow up that bank and cart the dirt down to the dam site. A hole was drilled in the bank and a stick of dynamite with fuse attached was placed in the hole. When the fuse was lighted we all scrambled across the logs to the other side and waited for the dynamite to blow the bank up.   One curious spectator to all this was a Chesapeake Bay retriever named Babs.   As soon as everyone ran, Babs proceeded to dig out the dynamite and came galloping down to the creek carrying the dynamite with fuse sputtering. Everyone was shouting at the dog and throwing rocks. Fortunately when he got to the creek the water put the fuse out. They tied Babs up before they re-set the dynamite.

(l-r) George Butcher and Myself (1939)

(l-r) Bill Burden, Ron Ullathorne,
Billy Walton (our version of the "Fonz"),
Myself, Jim Twiner (1939)

(l-r) Myself, Don LeVon, Stan North,
Billy Walton, Bruce LeVon (1940)

Chapter 8

One of my favorite memories of high school was the library and all the books available. By Christmas of my freshman year I had read seventeen books. Because of my paper route I could not go out for sports so I was automatically assigned to cross country running. Ninth and tenth grades were three mile distances and eleventh grade was for seven miles. If you had an "A" average in any subject you didn't have to take a final exam. The only finals I had to take were in Algebra.

When World War II started in 1939 my sister Myrtle married her sweetheart, John Todd, who as a Reservist was called up and left for England almost immediately. She would not see him again until May 1945.

In February 1941 when I turned eighteen I tried to enlist for pilot training in the RCAF. After a series of tests and physicals I was turned down due to color-blindness. I subsequently enlisted in the RCAF. On June 1st I went to school in St. Thomas to become an aircraft mechanic. There I met Lou Lemyre who became one of my lifelong friends. In order to get a weekend pass you either played in the band or played sports. Lou played in the band and I played any sport they had going so we could get a pass and hitchhike home to Toronto. We did this during the six months of school. We were scheduled to graduate on the 12th of December and had our orders for England when Pearl Harbor was attacked. Our orders were canceled and we were sent by train to Vancouver, B.C. On the train the weather was very bad and when we reached Edmonton it was 60 below zero when we stepped out on the platform. On reaching Vancouver we were sent to a Base called Jericho Beach. They did not even have rifles to arm us. Fortunately the Japanese never came. Then we were sent to Vancouver Island by ferryboat to Nanaimo and then by bus to Port Albirni on the west coast. From there we were supposed to go by boat to Ucuelet but the weather was so bad and the seas so rough we could not sail. We spent the next two nights in a Chinese restaurant waiting to sail. Finally on the third night the Captain decided he could make it and loaded everybody aboard on top of the supplies in the hold. There was not room for all of us so two had to stay on deck - Lou and I stayed behind the wheelhouse and we started out the channel in the dark to the open sea. When we reached the open waters waves started breaking over the bow and washing down the deck waist deep. Lou and I hung on to the mast behind the wheelhouse until after a while the weather calmed down. The people in the battened down hold were all seasick and it was a real mess down there. When we pulled in at the dock at Ucuelet the next morning we were a sorry looking bunch. The Station Sergeant Major, a Warrant Officer Cohen, was there to greet us. We overheard him tell the Orderly Room Clerk to take a ten-man detail from the new arrivals to unload the supplies. He was told to choose the men alphabetically which meant I was close to the top of the list. However, he started down the line taking names until he got to Lou Lemyre who wasn't going to take any chances so told them his name was Zilch. I was standing next to him and when he asked me my name I said Zilch but spelled with a 'p' - Zilpch. The clerk was very suspicious and copied the names as we gave them so we got out of the detail. Lou however had the nickname ``Zilch" throughout his military career.

Ucuelet was a flying boat base. The base had six Stranraer British flying boats. These were double winged with cross-struts and two engines. The planes were normally anchored out in the bay and only brought into the hangar for maintenance. We the maintenance personnel would wade into the water and attach beaching wheels to the plane so it could be pulled into the hangar. Another detail we had was guard duty at night on the planes that were anchored out on the water. The planes did anti-submarine patrols on the Canadian coast. It was decided that all personnel were to be given military training. A small Army detachment was brought in and set up a training course with ropes to climb and walls to climb over, water to wade through, barbed wire to crawl under. Each group got a week of instruction and the final test was to try to infiltrate the base without being caught.

When Lou and I finished our week of training, we took a boat that had a motor mounted on it for fishing and hid it up the bay. On the morning we were to infiltrate the base we had six people lying down in the boat and one person visible. They weren't expecting anyone to try to come in by boat, so seeing only one man in the boat they allowed it to come on the base. We jumped out of the boat and tossed smoke grenades into the hangars. We were the first to infiltrate the base.

In addition to the Strenraers we had two Blackburn Shark seaplanes. Orders came down to fly these two planes up north to Coal Harbour in the Queen Charlotte Islands. On the day these planes departed I was unaware that I had been assigned to fly in one of them. I had been working on a night shift and on that day had gone on a hike to Wreck Bay. There was an old character that lived in a shack there. He was known as Singapore Bill. At one time he had been on the police force in Singapore and had also prospected for gold in South America. He panned enough gold to keep him in groceries and scavenged whatever washed ashore on the bay. He was always giving us glass balls used by

Japanese fishermen to float their nets. These balls would be lost during storms and would reach the west coast of America after a two-year voyage.

On the way back to the base we began to notice some rather large paw prints on top of our foot prints we had made coming to the bay. The prints suddenly stopped under a large branch overhanging the trail. We had apparently walked underneath this mountain lion but it had not attacked. We were required to carry British Enfield rifles and eighty rounds of ammunition at all times. When we got back to the base I found out the shark seaplanes had departed and I had missed having to crew one of them. The next day we heard that one of the planes had crashed before reaching Coal Harbour.

When any plane was finished flying for the day the pilot would taxi the plane up to a refueling barge which was anchored out on the bay. Motorboats would whisk the crew to the base while we maintenance types refueled the plane, made our inspections and towed the plane to a buoy.

One day several of us were on the barge waiting to tow the plane. An aircraft electrician was inside the plane making his checks when we heard a splash, and immediately noticed one of the racks holding a depth charge under the wing was empty. Everyone made a mad scramble for motorboats shouting as they left to the electrician to get out of there. He finally stuck his head out of a hatch to find out what was going on. Fortunately the depth charge was set for a deeper level than where the gas barge was anchored. We immediately moved the plane and the gas barge. Next day some Canadian Japanese fishermen came and weighted a net with which they were able to bring up the depth charge.

By the fall of 1942 we started to receive Catalina type aircraft that had more range than the Stranraers. Came a day we finally had contact with the enemy. A Japanese submarine surfaced and began shelling our radio transmitter station. They had zeroed in on the radio transmissions they called the base for help. We had planes armed and ready but could not attack without headquarters approval in Ottawa. By the time Ottawa responded the submarine was gone. We were all infuriated at Ottawa. This same submarine later went south and shelled an oil refinery near San Diego.

(l-r) Art Waters and Myself
Stanley Park, Vancouver (1941)

Our transportation into Ucuelet
on a stormy night. (1941)

Myself in the cockpit
of a Fairy Battle aircraft.

Stranraer Flying Boat (1942)

Lou Lemyre and Penny North
sailing near our base. (1942)

Chapter 9

Around the first of December we received some overseas postings for England. Six of us aircraft mechanics departed on Christmas leave and reported to Halifax on the East coast of Canada on New Years day. The convoy we were scheduled to sail in was delayed because of a large number of German U-boat sightings. We were then sent back inland to Moncton, New Brunswick. A few days later we were on the train again heading south to the United States. We arrived at Camp Miles Standish in Taunton, Massachusetts. A few days later we went by train to New York and boarded the Queen Elizabeth. After a six day uneventful voyage we arrived in Glasgow Scotland. From there we went by train to Bournemouth on the south coast of England. In

Bournemouth the Canadian Air Force would sort out the new arrivals and then send them on the bases where needed. Sunday came and we were still in Bournemouth so we were separated, Catholics and Protestants and marched off to attend services in the local churches. Our group arrived at the front door of the Anglican Church. Two ranks filed in the door and down the center aisle. The church was full so when the first pair reached the altar, they did a right and left face and exited out two side doors of the sanctuary. The English congregation sat in stunned silence as Canadian airmen exited the church, leaped over the gravestones and headed back to town.

Assignments quickly followed. Eric Stofer, another mechanic named Johnny Simpson and myself was sent up to the Topcliffe, a base in the north of England in Yorkshire. Topcliffe was not an operational base but a base where crews who had been flying twin-engine bombers trained to fly the four engines Halifax bomber and pick up additional crewmembers. Topcliffe was sort of centrally located in Yorkshire with several nice towns within easy travel. My favorite was a town called Harrogate. On one occasion Johnny Simpson had gone to Harrogate without Eric or me to keep him out of trouble, which usually meant getting really drunk. On this night he reached that stage when the air raid sirens went off. The patrons of the pub where he was led him off to an air raid shelter. When he returned to base the next day all he could talk about was this gorgeous girl he had met in an air raid shelter. He had her name and address to prove it and a promise of a follow-up date next weekend with one stipulation. He had to bring a friend along for her gorgeous girl friend. After several days I finally relented and agreed to go with him. On Saturday we arrived in Harrogate, found the address he had been given and knocked on the door. The person who opened the door was a heavy-set woman who I assumed was probably the mother. As we were ushered into a sitting room we were both shocked as we realized this was the gorgeous creature he had met in a blackout in an air raid shelter. In the sitting room was another woman of even greater size. I'm sure both of them were looking back to age thirty while we were only twenty. We were introduced to the parents sitting in the kitchen and then left in the sitting room while the "girls" went upstairs to perform some miracle in make-up technology.

Our next move was to find a dark corner in a local pub and hope we would not run into anyone we knew from the Base. Things turned out okay after all. The girls were pleasant company. After a few beers and a dinner of bangers and mash (sausage and mashed potatoes) we made our excuses and caught a late train back to Topcliffe.

About a month later I was working on a plane out on the flight line when I spotted Eric and Johnny hurrying my way waving a piece of paper. "Bear, look what we took off the bulletin board in the hangar. They are short of flight engineers and are going to start a training course right here at Topcliffe." I reminded them we three had the same problem. We were color blind and could not qualify for air crew. "If they have a shortage of flight engineers maybe they won't care about that," said Eric. "Let's put our names down and see what happens."

I guess they had a real shortage because we were accepted to start training. Six weeks later we were flight engineers and promoted to Sergeant. As fate would have it all medical records reflecting our color blind condition had gone astray. We were quickly assigned to new crews coming to Topcliffe to train on Halifax bombers.

The crew I became part of all had at least five operational trips with the exception of the mid upper gunner. Our pilot, Bill Hingston, was a Canadian from Montreal. He was a McGill University graduate the most prestigious university in Canada. Howard Brown, the navigator was the oldest of our crew at thirty. At this time he had already completed twenty trips. On one occasion his crew was returning from the second of two trips in two days and his exhausted pilot crashed the plane on the runway trying to land. Brownie, as we called him, regained consciousness lying on the runway with the plane burning around him. He managed to pull the tail gunner out of what was left of a tail turret. They were the only survivors. Our bomb aimer was Jack Lockhead, RAF from Scotland. The wireless operator was also RAF. Taffy Williams was from Wales. He was the only married man on the crew. Our tail gunner, Novak, was from the Czechoslovakian Air Force who had managed to escape to England when the Germans occupied his country. The new mid upper gunner was Bob Hooper from St. Thomas in Canada. He was short, stocky with bright red hair. He had played high school football and shared my interest in listening to big band music. He was the youngest member of the crew. W started getting some training flights together as a crew. These were not without excitement sometimes. On one these flights Bill made a particularly hard landing causing the tail wheel to break off and go sailing through the air. This allowed the tail turret to drag the runway throwing up a shower of sparks. Our tail gunner on that turret was very upset about that landing. On another occasion we broke out of a cloud bank over the Irish Sea directly above a British heavy cruiser, who immediately started pumping anti aircraft shells in our direction. We fired off a flare with the colors of the day to indicate that we were a friendly aircraft, but they kept on shooting. The Isle of Man was close by and we watched an RAF Spitfire taking off from there to come and take a look at us. In a very short time we were declared combat ready and were transferred to the 429th Bomb Squadron at Leeming, Yorkshire about 25 miles from Topcliffe. Eric's crew and Johnny Simpson's crew were also assigned to the same squadron.

(l-r) SGT Dennis "Bear" Bruno, Flight Engineer, RCAF
F/LT Howard "Brownie" Brown, Navigator, RCAF
S/SGT Jock Lockhead, Bomb Aimer, RAF
P/O Bill Hingston, Pilot, RCAF
SGT Bob Hooper, Mid-Upper Gunner, RCAF
S/SGT Taffy Williams, Wireless Operator, RAF

Chapter 10

The Commander of the 429th Squadron was a Canadian. Wing Commander Patterson had done a tour as a fighter pilot and now wanted to try bombers. He wore a pair of pearl handled six guns much like General Patton and had some of Patton's temperaments. He wanted to fly on every mission but headquarters wouldn't let him.

On September 15, 1943 we went on our first mission as a crew. The target was a big rubber factory in Monlucon, France. The French underground said there was about a year's production of tires in the warehouses and the Germans were getting ready to start shipments to Germany. It was a bright moonlight night with two hundred planes attacking one factory complex that was several miles from Montlucon. When we arrived over the target it was already burning. Bill wanted to bomb a building that was not on fire so we dropped down lower and on the third pass found one and dropped our bombs. We climbed back up trying to regain as much altitude as possible before we reached the French coast where a lot of anti-aircraft fire could be expected. When we reached the coast we could still see the glow of the fires eighty miles away. Only six planes were lost on that raid.

The next night we got another French target, which was the railway tunnel at Modane on the French-Italian border. Because the long distance to the target meant carrying more gas, our bomb load was only five three hundred pound bombs. As we headed south we could see the lights burning in Switzerland while the lights in France were blacked out. We began experiencing a lot of icing on the wings and around the carburetor air intakes, making the plane difficult to handle. When we reached Modane we found the tunnel to be at the end of a valley surrounded by high mountains, making it hard to reach as a bombing target. With the plane still not handling well we made one run trying to line up on the tunnel and let the bombs go and banked out of there. By the time we got back to the English coast we were getting dangerously low on fuel due to the bad flying conditions. We called in on the radio asking for an emergency landing because we would be unable to reach our home base. We were directed to land at the American base at Thurleigh. After landing and being guided to a parking area we shut the engines down and climbed out. We were shocked to see that one of the three hundred pound bombs was still in the bomb bay of the plane. American bomb dolly equipment was too low so everyone left the bomb aimer and me to figure out how to get it off the plane. The bomb aimer got in the plane and started flipping switches while I stood with a long steel rod braced against the bomb in order to guide it into a bomb dolly if it did release. Finally we managed to lower the bomb and the rack it was mounted on.

We could not believe how good the American Air Force food was. At our base we were on English rations that were not to our taste so this was a real treat for us. The following day we refueled the plane and headed for Leeming. Before we could get there a fog bank rolled in making it impossible for us to land. We were diverted to another base at Yorkshire. Peering down through the thickening fog Bill called the tower for landing instructions. Given a runway number Bill proceeded to land fighting a heavy crosswind. When we touched down the wind pushed us off the runway and across a grass area towards the hangars. Up ahead of us was a bunch of English workmen digging a rather large ditch. Picks and shovels went flying as they scrambled to get out of the way of a Halifax bomber bearing down on them. When we reached the ditch, the under carriage collapsed on the left side spinning us to a stop. While this was happening, I threw all the magneto switches off, shutting down the engines. We hastily climbed out. Bill Hingston immediately spotted a pilot he knew among the onlookers. Doug Harvey had trained with Bill and they had gone their separate ways after training. "Harv, how are you? Any of the old crowd still with you?" He began talking about their training days, completely ignoring the base commander who had been standing there frustrated while Bill rattled on. "Sergeant, report to my office." Bill said, "Be there directly, Sir." And started talking to

Doug Harvey again. "NOW," roared the Wing Commander, his patience at an end.

Bill probably was not a great pilot. He may not even have been a good pilot, but he was our pilot. I think flying bored him because it was not intellectually stimulating. I never saw him exhibit any sign of fear in any situation.

Our plane was going to take a lot of repairing so we returned to Leeming by train carrying our parachutes and Mae West vests.

On September 29th we were briefed for an operation to Bochum Germany. We had a replacement aircraft which I did not like as much as our old one. It had the same Merlin engines except that one of them was a Packard Merlin made in the United States and did not have the power of the English built Merlin engines made by Rolls Royce. This plane could not get to eighteen thousand feet while our old one could almost make nineteen thousand. The French targets had lulled me into a feeling of safety. German targets where German fighter aircraft were numerous, skies filled with exploding anti aircraft shells, search lights turning night into day and seeing other aircraft burning and going down was another story.

On October 3rd we bombed Kassel. Losses were only 26 planes, which was light for a German target. I guess we did not do a very good job because on the 22nd of October they sent us back to Kassel. This time the losses were 48 planes. On November 28th we went to Ludwigshafen and again the losses were heavy. Four days later on November 22nd we were alerted for another operation. The briefing room was buzzing with guesses as to what the target would be. Wing Commander Patterson strode in and we were called to attention. Patterson wasted no time. He pulled the curtain revealing the target with the route in and the route home. An agonized groan went up when we viewed the map. We were going to Berlin. This was to be an 800-plane raid and our squadron would be in the first wave of two hundred planes. The weather people came on with their best guesses about broken cloud cover and light northeast winds. Intelligence people followed pointing out German fighter bases in the vicinity of our route. Single and twin-engine fighters at Stendal droned the briefing officer for intelligence and heavy anti aircraft defenses around the target area. We were a pretty somber bunch as we filed out of the briefing. Our crew had an additional concern. Our tail gunner Novak had been grounded. His alcoholism had gotten to be too much. His nerves were so bad he could not get in the plane unless he was under the influence. We were sorry to lose him because he was a good gunner. Our new tail gunner was Flight Sergeant Hamilton, a Canadian from Reynardton Nova Scotia. I only met him for the first time as we prepared for take off. We climbed out in solid clouds over the North Sea and headed south. Our route into Germany was over the Netherlands where we turned east. As we passed south of Hanover I was able to get a couple of bearings on Hanover for Brownie, the navigator, which gave him a good fix on our position. Brownie was concerned because wind speeds appeared to be different from what we had been given at briefing. Cloud cover continued to be pretty solid. We were nearing Berlin, or so we hoped, and nothing was happening. No anti aircraft fire, no search lights. Two minutes to our scheduled bombing time and nothing but clouds. Surely we were not off course and unable to find Berlin. One minute to bombing time, still nothing but clouds. Then suddenly directly in front of us a large red flare blossomed in the clouds followed by a shower of white flares. This was the method used by British pathfinder aircraft to mark targets at night. At the same moment the flare appeared every anti aircraft gun in Berlin commenced firing. We opened the bomb doors and seconds later our bombs fell through the lighted flares. We turned south out of the target area. We did not think we had sustained any damage. Our route home was a westerly heading and then a turn north over Belgium and over the North Sea again to England. We were still going west when we ran into very heavy anti aircraft fire. Searchlights snapped on and a couple of them actually coned us while we banked and weaved trying to get away from them. The starboard inner engine started to emit a trail of white smoke, which indicated the coolant system, had been hit and we were going to lose that engine.

An anti aircraft shell came through the floor of the aircraft and went through the tracks carrying ammunition to the mid upper gun turret causing a few rounds to go off in the aircraft and then it exited through the top of the fuselage leaving about a six inch hole. Apparently it was a dud shell. A lot of slave labor was used in Germany, some in the manufacture of munitions. Some of these people would deliberately do things to sabotage the munitions. I like to think that somebody helped us that night.

For about twenty minutes we ran through intense fire and we knew we had to be off course and over the Rhur Valley, the only area in Germany with this much firepower.

Looking at the fuel gauges I could see one of the fuel tanks on the starboard wing appeared to be losing fuel. By operating certain valves in the fuel lines and using a wobble pump, I started transferring gas to the tanks in the port wing. The starboard inner engine quit but we managed to feather the propeller so it would not create a drag. With my flashlight I could see oil streaks on the cowlings of the port inner engine and now the starboard outer engine was running rough. Bill Hingston noticed he was getting different readings between his gyro compass and his magnetic compass. Small variations occasionally occurred usually when something affected the magnetic compass. We were out of the Rhur but had no idea where we were and not too sure which direction we were going. Taffy Williams got busy on the radio calling England for a fix on our radio signal. Finally they answered and we found out we were now over Normandy and heading out into the Atlantic. With a change of course we started to pick up the Leeming beam which we followed up to Yorkshire. Fuel levels were getting dangerously low so we reported an emergency and asked to get diverted to the nearest runway available. We landed at Thalthorpe. The next day we went down to the hangar to look at our plane. Mechanics had picked seventy-three pieces of shrapnel out of various parts of the plane. One piece had damaged the gyrocompass and had been responsible for the incorrect compass readings. We must have picked that up over Berlin. The BBC reported that we lost 53 planes.

Wing Commander Patterson had asked Headquarters for permission to take the mid upper gun turrets off our squadron planes and install a small Plexiglas blister on the floor of the aircraft. The plan was to allow us to carry a bigger bomb load. The mid upper gunner was to lie on the floor and watch for fighters trying to attack from below, which was where most attacks were made. This was a very unpopular move, which the crews resented. We were already averaging two planes lost out of ten on every raid. In hindsight they now say a person would have been safer going ashore at Iwo Jima than being assigned to American or British bomber crews bombing Europe. On the 26th of November we went to Stuttgart. We quickly discovered problems with Bob Hooper having to lie on the floor, face down in a Plexiglas blister. Moisture from his breath dripped into his oxygen mask cutting off his oxygen. Bob's voice sounded slurred on the intercom so Bill told me to go back and check on him. Realizing what the problem was I put the spare oxygen mask that we carried on him and he was okay. I hung his mask on a heat vent and every thirty minutes gave him a dry mask. We got home safely but still unhappy over the loss of our mid upper turret.

A new concern had begun to worry our crew. Brownie now had twenty-nine trips and needed only one more to finish his tour. This meant that after the next trip we would be getting a new navigator, probably one that had just finished training. We didn't need any more problems.

Chapter 11

On the third of December we were alerted for another operation. A new pilot got to make two trips with an experienced crew before taking his own crew on an operation. A Canadian pilot Flying Officer Watson was to go along with us on his second trip. At the briefing the curtain over the map of Europe was pulled back to reveal Leipzig as the target. The route made it seem as if we were going to Berlin, but at the last minute we turned and went south to Leipzig. This would make everyone in Berlin go to the air raid shelters and lose a lot of sleep.

Eric Stofer and Johnny Simpson had returned from leave that day and were not scheduled to fly. They came out to where our aircraft was parked to see me off and wish me luck. I handed Eric my wallet and a small address book I had in my pocket for him to keep for me until I got back. Everything started off smoothly. We crossed the coast and over Germany turned east towards Berlin. We were nearing Brandenburg, the place where we would turn south, when a German fighter slipped up underneath us riddling the starboard wing with canon fire and starting a fire just behind the starboard inner engine. Bill was banking and weaving the place but the fighter was no longer visible. Our bomb load included some incendiaries so Bill decided to jettison the bombs. I went back to the middle of the aircraft and picked up my parachute and the one belonging to our second pilot. Bill had a seat type chute, which he was wearing. Watson had folded up the second pilot seat and was standing there when I clipped his chute on to his harness. Bill turned his head and said ``Bear, go back and see if you can tell what the hell is burning.'' He did not appear to be the least bit flustered. I unhooked my oxygen and intercom connection to my helmet and moved back to a small window overlooking the wing surface. I told him it might be an oil tank that was burning and the flames seemed to be spreading. Bill said "I guess we may as well bail out." Jock Lochhead came on the intercom and said "Skipper, I don't want to walk home from here, can we try diving and blowing the flames out?" Bill immediately stuck the nose down and dived the plane. I told him the flames were now over a gas tank that could blow up.

When he leveled out the flames were worse. "Okay guys, bail out," said Bill. Brownie told me later that he already had the front hatch open and had his feet sticking out when Bill gave the order to bail out. He had just cleared the aircraft when one of the wing gas tanks exploded forcing the starboard wing down. I was still back at the window overlooking the wing. Smoke and fumes filled the plane as we started to drop like a rock. The main hatch was now above my head and it opened easily. Bob Hooper was standing beside me and I told him "let's go" and pulled myself up in the open hatch. As soon as I was part way out the slipstream caught me and pulled me out. I pulled the release on my parachute and it snapped open. The plane disappeared in the clouds below with engines screaming. I felt like I was suspended in space. I heard the plane hit the ground and saw a brief gleam in the clouds below. I was really cold and in a state of shock, wondering how many of the crew had managed to bail out. I could hear ammunition rounds popping in the distance where our plane was probably still burning.

Suddenly I saw a blur of branches of a tree I had just missed. I had landed on the frozen ground of a plowed field. I sprained an ankle but was otherwise unhurt. Fog was so thick I could only see a very short distance. I could not bury my parachute because the ground was frozen, so I just stuck it under a bush. I climbed over a fence on to a road. There was a light layer of snow on the ground. I pulled out my escape kit, which we all carried and found a small compass because I had no idea which direction was north or south. The road seemed to be nearly east and west so I started walking west. I had only covered a short distance when some buildings became visible. Turning back a short distance I climbed over the fence on the north side of the road wanting to go around whatever buildings was up ahead. Every few feet I kept running into more fences. I had stumbled into the garden plots of a communal farm. The fences would squeak as I tried to get out of there. A dog started barking somewhere. I ended up getting back on the road and decided to risk passing the buildings. In the fog I saw two red dots and suddenly realized I was looking at the burning ends of two cigarettes. I make out the forms of two men standing in the doorway. One of them said something to me and appeared to be asking me about the "fligen machinen." I grunted at him and kept walking. I heard some more conversation and then heard a door slam. Out of the fog loomed a bigger barn-like structure. I found a door and went inside. I lit a match hoping to find some food of some kind I could take with me. There was only farm machinery of sorts so I left. Going west there was no more roads, just fields and wooded areas. I walked until it began to get daylight. The fog had now thinned and I was looking for some place I could hide. In the middle of a large field I saw a big straw stack. The outsides were wet and frozen so I could not dig into it. I managed to climb up on top and burrow down.

One thing that was really bothering me was that I had never told my mother that I was now a flight engineer and flying over Germany. I had thought to spare her that worry. Now she would receive a telegram from Ottawa saying I was missing in action. I was wishing that I had told her what I was doing. Then she would have been more prepared to receive that kind of news.

I checked over the items in the escape kit. German marks, French francs, a small map of Germany, a rubber water bottle, some water purification tablets, 30 Horlick tablets which were like vitamin tablets. Figuring it would take me at least 10 days to get to Holland or France, I decided to ration myself to three tablets each day. There were also two button compasses and a small file, a small chocolate bar and a safety razor with one blade. I also had a thirty-eight Smith and Weston revolver and four rounds. I settled down to take a nap but some noise caused me to peek out. Coming into the field were two horse drawn carts and a dozen farm workers carrying pitchforks. The carts were loaded with manure, which they started pitching out of the carts and spreading it on the ground. I was concerned that when they got close to my hiding place they would see where the straw was disturbed and I would be discovered. Amazingly they worked on by the stack without noticing anything. About a half hour later I heard some dogs barking. The barking continued and seemed to be getting louder. Suddenly it dawned on me they must have found my chute or had picked up my trail somewhere. The barking was really loud now and then I saw them. Two Doberman Pinschers and a German shepherd came out of the trees at the same place I had. When they got to the fence around the field they came through into the field. I started to panic. I surely didn't want to be chewed up by some dogs, but if I shot them their handlers would no doubt shoot me. But the dogs had stopped as soon as they entered the field. The manure was covering my trail and they had lost the scent. Minutes later three army types with rifles came into the field and leashed up the dogs. Meanwhile the farm workers had stopped working and were watching the dogs and the arriving army personnel. They in turn walked over to talk to the farmers. They then took the dogs and climbed through the fence and started following the fence line trying to pick up my trail where I came out of the field. It was a big field and it took them awhile to go completely around it and then they left. Nobody thought to check the straw stack.

The farm workers departed and when it started to get dark I headed west again. I broke the ice over some water in a ditch and filled my water bottle. I put in a purification tablet and shook it up. The water tasted terrible. About eight o'clock I came to a small village. It was a cold night and nobody seemed to be out so I took a chance and walked through it. The one road through it had a brick surface. There was a water pump on the street so I started pumping it to get some good water. The pump screeched loudly but no water was coming out. Thinking it might not be a working pump I hurried away before someone started wondering what idiot was trying to get water from a dry pump. My concern was to try and find something to eat. I looked in one out building hoping to find something. There was a woman's bicycle in there but it had a flat tire and there was no air pump. I left without finding anything.

When daylight came I found a stock shelter in a field and decided to spend the day in it. It was open on one side. There were no animals around. I knocked out a knothole on the blind side of the building so I could see any traffic on the road on that side. I lay down and dozed off. I awoke with a funny tingling sensation in my fingers. Two field mice were nibbling on my fingertips. They were as hungry as I was. After a restless day I started out walking while it was still daylight. I stayed off the road and was following a footpath across some open country when I saw a man on a bicycle coming toward me. There was nothing to do but keep walking like I belonged there. I had taken all the insignia and sergeant stripes off my Ike jacket and was wearing a white turtleneck sweater under it. I had also cut the top off my flying boots. They were made in such a manner as to appear to be regular shoes when the tops were removed. When I met the cyclist he called out a greeting in German. I waved an arm and grunted at him and kept walking. I was getting good at grunting in German. I don't remember too much about the rest of that night. The following day was spent in a grove of trees, close to a fairly busy road. I was still sticking to my three Horlick tablets a day. Hunger was steadily becoming more of a worry. That day I ate part of my chocolate bar. The following evening I saw some road signs showing distance in kilometers to different towns. I could not find them on my map. When daylight came I was just entering what appeared to be a forestry area. As far ahead as I could see were lines of pine trees. With such good cover I kept on walking. About an hour later I came to the end of the forestry area. I spotted a forest fire look out tower with a glassed in observation deck. I by passed it keeping out of the line of sight of the tower. There was an old shack near a clearing in the trees with the door hanging open. I heard a train whistle so I moved down to see where it was coming from. I was tired of walking and unable to find food. I decided to wait for dark and try to get on a train. The sun was shining for the first time since I landed in Germany. I went back up to the old shack, pulled the door down and lay in the sun. I had dozed off but some noise disturbed me. I looked up to see a girl on a bicycle disappearing into the trees at the bottom of the clearing. Thinking she had not seen me I pulled the door inside the shack and lay down again. I heard some voices and saw two uniformed men with rifles and a girl pushing a bicycle. She had seen me after all. They shouted something in German and I answered them in my high school French claiming to be a French worker. I understood what he said when he asked for my papers. It was all over. They marched me back to where I had seen the fire tower. There was a building there, which we entered. They sat me down at a table and one of them made a phone call. They had not searched me so I slipped my chocolate bar out and ate the rest of it. After a while I asked to go to the bathroom, which they understood. One of them escorted me out to an outhouse but would not let me close the door. I had hoped to dump the gun and the escape kit but could not with him watching. We had no sooner returned to the building when a staff car drove up. A German Air Force officer accompanied by two enlisted men carrying automatic weapons entered. The officer spoke perfect English. He asked me to empty my pockets. When he saw the escape kit items he took our some papers from his brief case and started checking off the items on a list that he had. He asked my name, rank and serial number which I gave him. He wanted to know where I came from because there had been no air raid for four days. I told him I could only give him my name, rank and serial number. He told me to strip because they had to check my clothes. I took off my Ike jacket and then I pulled the revolver from under my sweater and laid it on the table. I think when he first arrived he had congratulated the home guards for capturing me. Now he turned on them and had them standing at attention, giving them a tongue lashing for not searching me for weapons. Both army men gave me dirty looks and probably wished they had shot me. He emptied the shells from my Smith and Weston and chuckled. He said that it was a cowboy gun. "Let me show you a real gun" he said. He unbuckled his holster, removed the clip and handed me the Lugar. I told him I thought it was a nice gun. After getting my clothes back I dressed and then we departed in the staff car. We drove to the German air base at Stendal and went into an office. They brought me a bowl of soup and a large sandwich. I started on the soup, which tasted delicious. I had only finished about half the soup and I felt so full I could not eat any more. My stomach had shrunk. Little by little I would take another spoonful and eventually was able to finish it. They wrapped the sandwich up for me. I thanked the officer and left with the two enlisted men and a driver in the staff car. We drove to the railway station in Hanover. It was dark by this time and the station was crowded. The place seemed to be run by a different uniformed railway police. They wore a big metal plate on a chain over their chest and spent their time blowing whistles and directing people about. I had my sandwich but my two guards needed something to eat so we went into a military canteen. We sat down at a table and then they went up to the counter to get some food. About that time I was approached by what appeared to be a very angry uniformed person screaming at me in German. My guards quickly intervened and explained my presence. They told me later that he was a member of an elite mountain ski unit. After awhile we boarded a train. The conductor cleared some passengers out of a compartment and we went in and sat down. Some of the people who had been closed out were now allowed to return and take the vacant seats.

SGT. BRUNO MISSING IN AIR OPERATIONS

Served as Flight Engineer With Four-Engined Bomber Squadron

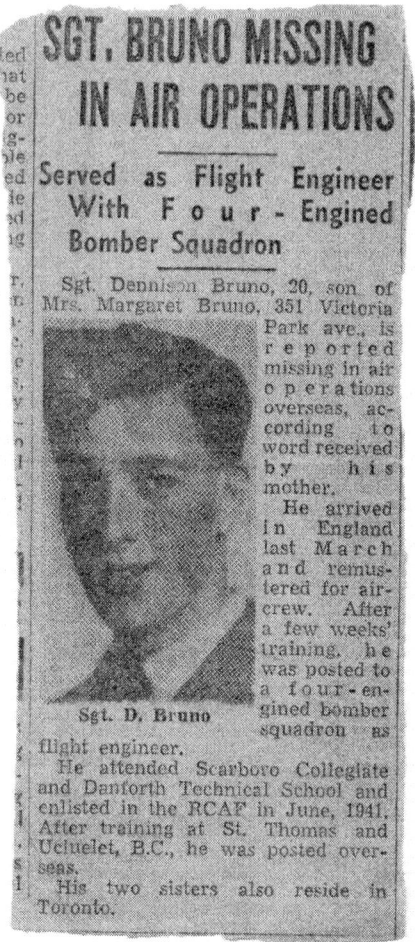

Sgt. Dennison Bruno, 20, son of Mrs. Margaret Bruno, 351 Victoria Park ave., is reported missing in air operations overseas, according to word received by his mother.

He arrived in England last March and remustered for aircrew. After a few weeks' training, he was posted to a four-engined bomber squadron as flight engineer.

Sgt. D. Bruno

He attended Scarboro Collegiate and Danforth Technical School and enlisted in the RCAF in June, 1941. After training at St. Thomas and Ucluelet, B.C., he was posted overseas.

His two sisters also reside in Toronto.

MIA story in the Toronto newspaper. (1943)

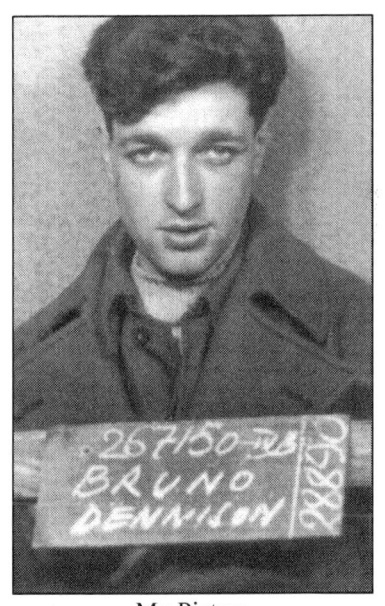

My Picture
Taken from German Files
Prison Camp: Stalag IV B

Chapter 12

In the morning we arrived at Frankfurt. I was ushered into the interrogation center and my guards left. I was placed in a cell that was about eight feet long and about five feet wide. It had a cot on one wall. There was a small barred window with frosted glass. The door had a peephole the guards could open to look in and a lever, which operated as a signal in the hall if you wanted to go to the bathroom. This cell was frigid cold most of the time but once in while they turned on the heat and it was extremely hot.

The next day I had a visit from a strange looking character wearing a Red Cross emblem on his arm. Back in England we had been briefed as what to expect if we were taken prisoner. In England this person was known as ``Creeping Jesus." With glasses that looked like bottoms of Coca Cola bottles. He handed out forms he wanted me to fill out ``so your family would know you were safe". The forms asked for information about your squadron, type of plane, bomb load, target etc. When a prisoner did not fill out the forms he would threaten that the Gestapo would get the information one way or another. Three days went by and I was taken to a room to be interviewed. My interrogator talked with a New York accent and had a pretty secretary in a short skirt on hand to take notes. He offered me a cigarette and proceeded to ask the same questions as before. Again I was threatened and told I would be turned over to the Gestapo. In the meantime I was sent back to my cell. The next morning a guard opened my door and standing there with him was Brownie. He was as shocked to see me as I was to see him.. Brownie apologized saying he had given the Germans the names of all of the crew because he had seen the plane blow up and just knew that nobody else could possibly have gotten out. He had done this thinking that it would be easier for all the crewmember's families if they knew their loved ones were dead. We did not talk any more because we figured the Germans were listening to what we were saying. They took Brownie away.

A couple of days later I was taken to a compound called Dulag Luft. My flying boot type shoes were replaced by American army brogans, and I was given my first Red Cross parcel. Brownie was still there so we got to talk privately. He talked about having his feet hanging out of the hatch waiting for the order to bail out. His feet were frozen and he landed hard hurting his back. He was in extreme pain but managed to get out to a road, rolled himself in his chute. Some farm workers found him the next morning. When they found out he couldn't walk they got a cart and took him to one of their homes. They got him into a chair and put his feet in an oven. He was better now but still in a lot of pain. Since Brownie was an officer he was sent to a different camp than I was. I would not see him again until we got back to England. The next day I was taken with a bunch of other prisoners to the railway yards in Frankfurt. On the way we had stopped at an intersection where a column of barefoot women and children were trotting along under guard.

Somebody in our group who could speak some German called out to them and asked them who they were. "Polski" was the reply from one of the women. Apparently they were Polish slave laborers.

At the railway yard we were loaded into box cars. There were so many people in each boxcar there was no room for everyone to sit down at the same time. We traveled east at a slow pace. We were shunted to sidings a lot.

After three days we arrived at Muhlberg in East Germany. We left the train and marched almost three miles to Stalag IV-B. The camp was a large complex of fenced compounds. There were over fifteen thousand prisoners in the camp, most of which were Russian. There were also a large number of French and Italian. At the time of my arrival there were only a handful of Americans in this camp. This would change later on. British prisoners were the next largest group including a few hundred air force personnel. Smaller groups from almost every country in Europe, including the Danes and the Dutch, made up the rest. Our barracks was one large room with about one hundred and fifty prisoners. There was a washroom at one end with one cold-water tap. Another barracks adjoined the washroom. Each barracks had a stove in the middle but very little fuel such as coal or wood was available. Most food was warmed up on small home made blower units made out of tin cans out of Red Cross parcels and bits of wire. A few scraps of paper and wood fueled these. Our guards were older veterans most of whom had been wounded during service on the Russian front. They were probably happy to be camp guards. German rations were based on what we called 'skilly', which was a cabbage soup with added ingredients such as rotting potatoes and sometimes horsemeat. They must have used every bit of the horse except the hide and the hoofs because it was not uncommon to get eyeballs or teeth.

We had arrived in the camp a few days before Christmas 1943. On Christmas Day the Camp Commandant doubled the bread ration. We thought that was a very nice gesture but the following week our bread ration was reduced. We heard that the Commandant had exceeded his authority to double the bread ration so it had to be made up by shorting later rations.

As NCOs' we were not required to do any work except camp maintenance. About once a month there was one detail we could participate in. A group of prisoners with guards would go out of the camp to a wooded area where we could pick up any dead branches and carry back to the camp. Escape attempts were forbidden on this detail because we would no longer be allowed to gather wood if anyone tried to escape. Red Cross parcels were real lifesavers. From one parcel every two weeks they became more and more scarce. Cigarettes were the monetary unit in the camp. Some enterprising guys set up a stand where you could trade items from your Red Cross parcel for other items or for cigarettes. They had a chalkboard, which showed the price of different items in cigarettes. They also bought and sold rings, watches and fountain pens. If parcels came in, prices dipped. No parcels and prices went up.

One thing that really upset the Germans was the fact that we had a radio in the camp capable of tuning in on the BBC from England. Every day the news broadcast was copied and posted on a bulletin board for any to read. The Germans made repeated searches trying to locate that radio. Sometimes we would play tricks on the Germans. We would run a length of wire down the side of one of the barracks as if it were an antenna. Some sharp-eyed guard would spot the wire and report it. A truckload of guards would roar into camp, surround that particular hut and search for the radio. At the end of the wire would be a tin can with a note saying "It's not here." This, of course, upset them and they would trash the inside of the hut while we whistled and jeered. The radio was actually hidden under the bass keys of a piano accordion. As the war progressed, even the German guards would slip up and read the news.

I was not aware for quite a while that some of the prisoners had started digging an escape tunnel. The closest building to the outside fence in the British compound was one used as a library. A row of bookshelves that could be pushed back covered the entrance into the tunnel. Bed board slats were used to shore up the sides and ceiling. Everyone ended up sleeping on four or five bed boards with big gaps in between. This was a volunteer effort. I had done all the walking I wanted to do and knew the chances of covering such a long distance to Switzerland or France was slim. They continued to dig and the tunnel passed under the outside fence. They were angling the tunnel up towards the surface when a large chunk fell in right on the pathway used by the guards to patrol the fence. The first guard to come along gave the alarm. The "honey cart" that was used to pump and carry off the contents of our central latrine was now used to fill the tunnel. The Camp Commandant was very complimentary on the engineering that had gone into constructing the tunnel but he closed the library.

Some of the people in the camp had truly remarkable stories. Two New Zealand brothers both ended up at Stalag IV-B. Alex Shand joined the New Zealand army. He was captured at Tobruk in North Africa and came through the Italian camps to Muhlberg. His brother John worked for British Overseas Airways and was in London when the war broke out. He enlisted in the RAF, was shot down and was sent to Muhlberg.

Another remarkable New Zealander was Sergeant Jack Ward. He was captured in North Africa and sent to a camp in Italy. During an escape attempt he killed a

German officer. He was able to escape and linked up with an Italian underground Communist cell that was blowing up bridges and railways etc. One in the group turned him over to the Germans who shipped him to Germany for a trial for killing a German officer. They intended to find him guilty and put him before a firing squad. When he arrived at our camp he was allowed to take a shower. While in the shower he managed to pull a water pipe off the wall and use it to pry the bars on a window. He escaped from the shower building and ran naked into the British compound. The Germans immediately mounted repeated searches of the camp but could not find Sgt. Ward. He survived to go home after the defeat of Germany. An interesting character was the one Norwegian prisoner, Paul Molvik. When Finland was invaded by Russia, Paul volunteered to fight for Finland. When war started in the rest of Europe Paul was awarded the Mannerheim Medal by Finland and allowed to go home to defend Norway. He was stationed on the island of Spitsbergen off the north coast of Norway and was captured by the Germans when they occupied the island. He was marched the length of Norway and ended up in our camp. I feel privileged to have known the likes of these people.

Chapter 13

After D-Day our spirits soared. From then on we started getting American prisoners into the camp. Some stayed and some went on to other camps. After the Battle of the Bulge several thousand Americans came through. As the eastern and western fronts edged closer we began to see more things happening. Twice America Thunderbolt aircraft made a strafing run on our camp, realized their error and left. On another occasion they caught a German train loaded with naval shells on the railway just east of our camp. This was the main Berlin to Dresden line. On the first pass the planes took out the engine and an anti-aircraft flat car. The gunners fired twice at the planes, then started running. The planes started fires in some of the cars and the shells started exploding. Standing in the camp watching this show it felt like a blow to the stomach every time one of those cars exploded. Twenty-four hours later the Germans had the line cleared and the trains were running again.

A new and different shipment of prisoners arrived in our camp. Russian forces were now within a few miles of Warsaw. Polish freedom fighters in the city attacked the Germans expecting the Russians to come on in. Instead of pushing on into Warsaw the Russians stopped and allowed the Germans to wipe out the outnumbered Poles. The prisoners arriving in our camp were several hundred Polish women and children from Warsaw. They were isolated in a separate compound.

Artillery on the eastern front, which had started as a distant rumble, became louder every day. On the 29th of April we had no morning head count. None of the guards were visible and we wondered what was happening. A few minutes later, three men on horseback rode up to the gate. They were Russian Cossacks with rifles slung across their back. They opened the main gate and rode into the camp. A mob of Russian prisoners surged forward surrounding the new arrivals. Screaming and shouting they punched and pawed the new arrivals. More Russians started arriving and the camp was in an uproar. One of the first things the Russian prisoners did was to identify those prisoners who had cooperated with the Germans. They were quickly lined up and shot. The Russians had no food for over twenty thousand prisoners. We would be allowed to search an area of 25 kilometers around the camp for any food items. We were warned not to go west towards the Elbe River or we would probably be shot. Russian forces were trying to prevent German stragglers from getting across the Elbe where they would have a chance to surrender to American army units. In one day the area was stripped of all food. The German populace that had not been killed was left with no food. We came across a farm family, a man a woman and two children hanging from a tree. Germany was paying for their brutal treatment of the Russians.

After a few days the Russians decided to move us to the town of Risa on the west side of the Elbe. We walked all day behind an escort of Russian tanks. In Risa they put us into a German military compound that had a high brick wall around it. We still had no food so the next morning I went over the wall along with four Australian air force friends. After wandering around for a while we noticed a house where the front door was ajar. We looked inside and discovered the bodies of an elderly couple. The only food we found was a head of cabbage. The back door opened and a young German girl slipped in. Arthur Ashley, one of the Australians spoke German and ascertained that the dead couple was her parents. She promised to return after dark with some friends to take her parents for burial. She also promised to bring us some food at that time. When they came we helped load the bodies into a cart. She told us she had heard on the radio that Germany had surrendered. The date was the seventh of May.

On the eighth we woke up to the sound of a lot of small arms in the area. A couple of military vehicles came along in the street with Russians singing and waving bottles. Another vehicle turned into the street and the Russian occupants were spraying the front of the houses with automatic rifle fire. We lay on the floor with glass falling from the windows above us. We spent the rest of the day keeping out of sight and listening to the sound of gunfire. The next morning the town was silent and the streets were empty. On the edge of town we came to a field with a huge heap of bicycles and carts piled up. The Russians had been taking them away from the refugees coming in from the east. There were two Russian guards sprawled on the ground either asleep or passed out, we quietly selected some bicycles and rode away.

We headed west hoping to reach the American lines. We met a smart looking Russian infantry unit marching and singing. Some of them stopped and tried to take our bicycles. There was a lot of pulling and shoving. A Russian officer came up and said something and they left us alone. A hare jumped up in a field and one of the Russian sprayed him with a sub machine gun to the cheers of his comrades. That night we stayed at a farm house. There appeared to be only women there who begged us to stay saying the Russians would not bother them if we were there. During the night some drunken Russians did show up. They pushed on the door and true to what the women had said they left after seeing us there.

The next day we came to a river and the bridge had been destroyed. We followed the riverbank and came to a railway bridge. It had also been destroyed but some of the girders were still visible above the water. Carrying our bicycles we managed to climb across. Back on the road again we came to a building where a lot of singing and drinking were going on. The women there were French slave labor whose prison serial numbers were tattooed on their arms. We had a glass of wine and then went on our way. Our road led us to an autobahn where we met our first Americans. A jeep with four Americans stopped and told us to go on into Leipzig. They had no food to give up but did give us a cigarette.

Continuing on we came to a fork in the autobahn. Standing there was a German who had only one arm and was wearing a German uniform jacket. We asked him which fork went to Leipzig and in good English he gave us directions. He asked us if we were hungry and when we said "yes" he said to follow him. He took us about a half a mile to a winery complex and introduced us to his father the owner and his mother. The family's name was Bruno the same as mine and they had an interesting story.

The father had been in England on business and had married an English girl. They had two sons and continued to stay in England. In 1938 his brother had died in Germany and he had inherited the winery. If they sold the winery the Germans would only allow them to take ten shillings out of the country, so they elected to stay and keep the winery instead. After war broke out the following year they were trapped. Both sons were drafted into the German army. One lost his life on the Russian front and the other lost an arm. They wined and dined us. He said the Germans took their wine production every year but otherwise left them alone. When we left the next morning I gave them my Canadian address so we could get in touch after the war. In Leipzig we got a shower, a bunk to sleep in and a pass to get in the mess hall.

A couple of days later an American C-47 flew us to Brussels where we were turned over to the British. A flight the next day took us to an airport near London. I said goodbye to my Australian companions and got on a train to Bournemouth. There I met Brownie. He was leaving to go to London with the intention of getting married. He asked me to be the best man at his wedding to which I agreed. He could not give me directions to his fiancée's house but would meet me at a pub we both knew a week from Saturday. In the meantime I got ready to go up to London where some of us were scheduled to go to Buckingham Palace and have tea with the Queen. I checked into a hotel in London but was not feeling well. My eyes and skin had a yellow tinge and I could not keep any food down. I was determined to keep going until it was time to meet Brownie. Finally I woke up one morning and could not get out of bed. I called the desk and asked them to notify the Canadian Air Force that I was ill and to come and get me.

They took me to a Canadian Army Hospital in Watford outside of London. Hepatitis accounted for the yellow eyes and yellow skin. While in the hospital I also developed mumps. Now I was yellow with big lumps on my neck. Not a pretty sight. Six weeks later I was released and given a two-week leave. I went to Scotland by train to visit my Aunt and cousins and then back to Bournemouth. I found out I had been promoted to the rank of Pilot Officer (2nd Lieutenant).

We sailed from Liverpool bound for Canada. Somewhere out in the middle of the Atlantic we missed hitting a floating mine by about twenty-five yards. The ship was brought to a stop a safe distance away from the mine and they were going to try to detonate it with a rifle. The plan changed when they found out there was a British navy ship in the vicinity, so the mine position was reported to them to take care of the situation.

When I came through Montreal I tried to visit our pilot's mother. She lived in what appeared to be an expensive high-rise apartment. The doorman told me she was away at her summer home and did not know when she would return. I caught a train for Toronto.

Chapter 14

It was good to be home. My brother-in-law, John Todd, had made it home ahead of me after being overseas five and a half years. As an engineer he had worked in London during the blitz digging people out of bombed buildings and removing bombs that had not exploded. He went into France after D-Day and did a lot of clearing of mine fields. His nerves were bad and he would have problems the rest of his life. He did find a job he liked with Canada Wire and Cable Company.

I also traveled to St. Thomas to see the family of our mid upper gunner, Bob Hooper. That was a heart wrenching experience. They could not understand how I was alive and their son was not. After that experience I did not want to contact any other crew families. Jimmy

Steele, a good friend in Stalag IV-B lived in Toronto and was getting married. I did get to be best man at the wedding. I had written to Brownie explaining why I never showed up in London for his wedding but my letter came back stamped "address unknown."

I could not settle down. With a lot of back pay I partied every night. I bought a 1935 Chevrolet but the engine was so worn the spark plugs would foul up any time I climbed a hill or grade. I had been on leave for only a couple of weeks when the Air Force contacted me to find out if I wanted to volunteer for the Pacific theatre. The plan was to send Canadian crews to Kentucky to train on B-29's. I had never been to Kentucky so I said yes. The Air Force was still letting me live at home and check into a local base once a week when the war ended. Canada immediately decided to cut back on the size of its armed forces but did not know how much to cut. They decided on some reduction and to keep an interim force for two years. If I wanted to stay in I would be reduced to the rank of Flight Sergeant and could expect duty in the Northwest Territories of Canada where fighter plane bases were being developed to guard against Russian encroachment.   I did not relish duty in the Northwest Territories so I decided to take my discharge.

In October I was discharged and went to work for Warwick Brothers, a wholesale stationery company. Another friend, Jack Gray, wanted me to go into business with him by opening an appliance store. We never did get a franchise from any of the big appliance manufacturers. We did open a store concentrating on radio repair and installing car radios. We sold small appliances and lamps also.   For almost a year we struggled. Some weeks we made money; some weeks we lost money and finally closed down. Jack Gray's father had a tobacco store in which he decided to build a lunch counter and open for breakfast and lunch. He hired Jack and me to work there. This was quite successful.

Chapter 15

In September of 1947 the United States Air Force became a separate branch of the service from the Army. I had not seen much of the States. Jack Gray and I had made a trip to New York City where he had an aunt and uncle. I liked the States and decided to check with recruiting in Buffalo. I filled out a lot of papers and requested pilot training. It took awhile but by the last week of January 1948 I was back in Buffalo ready to be inducted. Recruiting put me up in a hotel in downtown Buffalo. The hotel was jammed. An ice skating revue had rented all available rooms. The front desk called my room to say they had a U. S Navy chief who needed a place to stay and would I mind sharing my room with him. When I agreed he came up to the room. He was an interesting guy. He had his own staff car and was touring navy installations giving instructions in some new program. This was on a Friday and I had to wait until Monday before taking the train to New York City where I would be inducted. This navy chief immediately started trying to recruit me into the navy. With a weekend and nothing to do we decided to drive back to Toronto.

So in his navy staff car we went to Toronto. I phoned a couple of girls I knew and we went dancing. On Sunday we drove back to Buffalo. We said goodbye and I left for New York City on Monday. Recruiting was in a rough section of the city. I remember seeing a naked man passed out on the sidewalk while pedestrians walked around him with hardly a glance. I lingered to see what would happen and after awhile a police van drove up and loaded him into the vehicle. I spent one night on Ellis Island in order to get a retake on a test. Duly sworn in, about twenty-five of us were put on a train bound for San Antonio, Texas where I started basic training.

It did not take our Flight Marcher very long to find out I had previous military experience. His regular assistant had gone off to California to bring back a prisoner so he appointed me to march the flight to the different classes we had to attend. This allowed our Flight Marcher to spend a lot of time in the NCO club.

On one particular day our Flight had KP duty in one of the mess halls. We were cleaning up after the last meal of the day when the mess sergeant on duty informed me he had a big inspection the following day and he had a long list of things he wanted cleaned. I told him we also had an inspection in the morning and had to clean our barracks after we left the mess hall. "Tough Luck" he said, "his mess hall came first." I walked away and called our Flight Marcher at the club and explained the problem. He told me when the troops had finished the regular KP duties to march them out of there. I passed the word for everyone to fall in on my signal. When everything was cleaned we quickly formed up and marched off, with one irate mess sergeant screaming at us. We had only gone a couple of blocks when an Air Police jeep with the Officer of the Day, pulled up and stopped the flight. He told me to march the men back to the mess hall. When we got there the Officer of the Day asked me if I knew the penalty for mutiny and disobeying an order by a non-commissioned officer. I told him I was just following the orders of our Flight Marcher and gave him the phone number where he could be reached to verify his instructions. The officer talked on the phone for a while and then came back and told the mess sergeant that these men had been on duty since five o'clock this morning and were now leaving and he suggested that the mess sergeant get busy and get his mess hall cleaned up because he was going to make it a point to see it was clean in the morning.

I had other troubles just getting through basic training. Everyone had to fill out a very detailed form for a background check. Since I was not yet a citizen and had lived in a few foreign countries, my form created a lot of interest. I was called in for an interview and questioned about what I had written down. Then they called me in again and said they had lost my form and I would have to make out a new one. When I was finished one of my interrogators took the form to another desk where I could see he was comparing it with what must have been my original form. This upset me and when he came back they started to question my politics and asked if I was a member of the Communist Party. By this time I was really angry and stood up and told them if they did not want me in the United States Air Force to say the word and I would go back to Canada and I walked out. I never heard any more from them. Near the end of our training I still did not know if I would be accepted for Pilot training as my enlistment form had indicated. Now they said that this was not possible because I was not a citizen. One personnel man told me to arrange a marriage with an American girl and I could then be a citizen in a year and could apply again. The alternative was that since I had been recruited under a false premise of training, paper work would be sent to Washington to approve a discharge. They estimated that could take up to a year and in the meantime I would stay at Lackland as an assistant Flight Marcher. The other alternative was to do my three-year enlistment. I chose the latter. By now everyone had follow up school assignments except me. As a result after basic I was shipped to Biggs Air Force Base in El Paso, Texas as unassigned.

Biggs put in for a school quota for aircraft maintenance for me and in the meantime I went to work on the flight line. The planes were B-26 twin-engine bombers and the Squadron was part of the 12th Air Force.

I went over to Juarez Mexico to do a little shopping, as I wanted to send a gift home to my mother. I was told before I went across the border not to pay what they asked but offer half the price and bargain from there. When I found a tablecloth with eight napkins that looked nice I asked the price. As instructed I offered half and eventually we reached an agreed price. When I got back to the barracks I proudly showed off my purchase only to find out I had only four napkins instead of eight. That was my first lesson in foreign exchange.

One Friday morning I awoke with someone telling me to report to the Orderly Room. When I got there they informed me they had a mandatory quota to fill for someone to go to teletype maintenance school at Scott Field in Illinois and that I had been selected to go. I told them I had aircraft maintenance assignment to school the following month. That would be canceled because I had to go on this new school quota. Unhappy with the latest turn of events I went to see the Base Inspector General to appeal this assignment. He checked into the matter and told me I had to leave today because my new school assignment started next Tuesday. He told me not to flunk out or I would never get another school and when I got back he would get me into an aircraft maintenance school. By this time it was after noon and Base Finance was already closed so I could not get any travel expense payment. Having decided to go I had enough of my own money to travel on and all I needed was a set of orders authorizing the travel. Biggs Air Base was on summer working hours and the base closed at 3:00 P.M. The Squadron Duty Officer and I finally got some orders printed up. I packed my duffle bag and went to the Greyhound Bus station in El Paso and booked travel to St. Louis. That was a miserable trip. Children sticking candy in my hair, babies crying and no air conditioning made for a sleepless trip. I arrived in St. Louis on Sunday afternoon and staggered around the corner from the bus station to a hotel and checked in. When I awoke it was noon the next day. I caught a bus to Scott Field and checked in on time to start school the next day.

Chapter 16

I found the teletype maintenance course very interesting, but two things detracted from the training. One was KP duty, which we were required to do about once a month. You missed the training your class got and had to pick up whatever they had covered on your own. The other problem was grass-cutting details. Scott Field had a lot of grass and only a handful of push mowers and a plethora of what we called idiot sticks. These were just rough sticks with a blade across the bottom, which you swung in an arc. The other grass trimming method was to line up on our hands and knees and pull the grass by hand. This was a demoralizing detail. Marching back to the barracks after one of those details we would all drag one leg as if we were on a chain gang. We did this while passing Base Headquarters and were sorely chastised because the General didn't like it.

While I was at Scott the Air Force decided that all the white two story barracks we lived in should be painted pastel colors to make them feel more like home. The various colors of paint were delivered in fifty-gallon drums to each barracks, as this was a self-help project and each squadron would paint their own buildings. One Monday morning we looked over to see that an adjacent squadron had painted all their buildings over the weekend. Our Commander took note of this and said we had to paint ours that week or we would be kept there over the weekend to paint. This got everyone's attention and by Friday we had all painted our own barracks. At the afternoon formation our Commander pointed out a problem. At the far end of our buildings was one barracks that was empty and had not been painted. When it was finished we would be free for the rest of the weekend. About a hundred people with brushes and coffee cans of paint were soon shoulder-to-shoulder tossing cans of paint on to the building and brushing it down. In twenty minutes the building, including door and windows, was an oozing mass of paint. We waited about a half hour and then selected one person who did not have too much paint on his clothes to tell the Commander we were finished. The Commander came out from his office and peered down the row of barracks to the one we had just finished. At such a distance the barracks looked great, so we were released for the weekend. A couple of weeks later a new influx of students were moved into this barracks. They were busy trying to free up doors and windows so they would open, and were scraping the windows with razor blades.

Eating in the big consolidated dining halls was reminiscent of some old prison movies. We sat on three legged wooden stools to eat. On a second level overlooking the dining areas were glassed in offices and a catwalk. Half a dozen columns of students filed along serving lines into the dining area. What ever went on your tray you were expected to eat. As you left you could scrape your tray into a refuse barrel and pass your tray into a window for washing. Spotters on the catwalk overhead would watch to make sure you were not throwing away food. A voice on a microphone would boom out something like "You there, eat that square of butter." To avoid this kind of hassle diners would surreptitiously scrape food they did not eat onto the floor under the table where they were sitting. I remember being on KP there and one of the KP pushers told us to go back to the freezer and chop up a block of ice. We did find a hatchet there so we chopped the ice and left it on the floor. The same KP pusher saw us and asked where the ice was. We told him in the freezer so he told us to bring it out. The floor was dirty but we scraped all the ice into a metal container and carried it out. The KP pusher grabbed it away from us, climbed a stepladder and dumped it into the ice tea urn. We watched for any friends coming through the food lines and told them not to drink the ice tea.

Finally graduation time came. I was the honor student in our class and got to meet with the General. When he asked for suggestions to improve their operation I mentioned the KP problem and the grass cutting. I could tell he really did not want to hear any criticism.

Because of incorrect wording in my travel orders, finance would not pay me any travel money, so once again I paid my own way hoping to straighten this matter out when I got back to Biggs. This time I went by train from St. Louis and changed trains in Dallas. On the train out of Dallas the conductor came through asking for tickets. When he looked at my ticket he told me this train does not go to El Paso. It only goes as far as Monahans. I had no idea where Monahans was but he said another train would come through there about six o'clock and I could continue on it. In Monahans I tried hitch hiking but no one was going as far as El Paso so I went back to the train station. Back on the train we were finally pulling into El Paso when the train hit a car at a level crossing. It was now close to eleven P.M. and I was supposed to report in before midnight. I left the train and started walking into El Paso. Eventually I found a cab and made it to the base with five minutes to spare. The next morning I was surprised to learn the Squadron that had sent me off to school had been deactivated and no longer existed.

The only organization on Base belonging to the 12th Air Force was the First Tow Target Squadron. Since I was a 12th Air Force asset that is where I was sent.

They did not have any teletype machines, so I went back to working on airplanes.

My new job was unpacking small single engine PQ aircraft from a crate. They had been stored for some time so we had to change out gaskets in carburetors, fuel pumps etc. We also installed a set of controls so the plane could be remotely controlled by radio signals from a mother ship. It could then be flown over the firing range on Fort Bliss where army anti-aircraft units would shoot it down.

A certain Major would come to the hangar almost every day to watch us work. We got to talking and I found out he was also a 12th Air Force asset that had been turned over to the 1st Tow Target Squadron. He had come to the base a few months ago and had been in charge of the Officer's Club operation. An inspection of the Officer's Club had revealed a large amount of money missing. A lowboy vehicle was taken up to the base commander's house on the mountain in El Paso and had brought back refrigeration units and other air force property. They had wanted the major to pay a small fine so they could close out this investigation but he refused to admit any wrong doing. The Base Commander, in the meantime, had been transferred to Hawaii.

I went to base finance to try to collect some of the travel pay I had coming. Since the organization that had issued the travel orders no longer existed they would not reimburse me. They said I would have to take it up with 12th Air Force. On the last Sunday of 1948 I drove one of the base chaplains up to the base at White Sands, New Mexico where he was to hold Sunday services. The sun was shining as we left El Paso, but high winds and blowing sand reduced visibility. When we arrived the wind made getting the chapel door open a real struggle. On the way home it started to rain. The combination of blowing sand and rain ruined the windshield of the car. Then it turned into snow. Back in El Paso there were several inches of snow on the ground. Since the base seldom had this kind of weather, it was not prepared. The coal burning furnaces in the barracks had no coal available. Wind blew in through cracks around windows and doors and left a white and brown layer of snow and sand on clothing racks and bunks. The guys in the barracks said the bad weather probably had something to do with my going to church that day.

Chapter 17

Someone in 12th Air Force Headquarters realized they had a teletype mechanic at Biggs Air Force base with nothing to do and they needed one there at Brooks Field in San Antonio. This time I made sure finance paid me in advance for my travel to San Antonio.

When I arrived, the teletype maintenance section was very glad to see me. It had recently lost some people and had only two mechanics left. The man in charge was an alcoholic ex-paratrooper and one other airman named Whitehead from Dennison, Texas. The base had a good-sized message center, a weather center in base operations and a pony circuit to the Base Commander's office. Our Sergeant in charge did not do any maintenance work but did order and stock a good supply of spare parts.

Whitehead and I would take turns checking out a truck from the motor pool before seven A.M. We worked from 7 to 5 and then washed the truck and turned it in to the motor pool. Between us we did all the maintenance. One of us had to be on call at night and on weekends. Needless to say we stayed busy and put in a lot of hours.

There were a couple of guys on the Base I became good friends with. One was named Sullivan from Boston. Before coming into the Air Force he had made a living as a pool hall hustler. Everyone knew not to play pool for money with him. The other one was names Carter. He had a private pilot's license. One weekend he rented a plane and we flew to a dude ranch that catered to people with airplanes. When you landed, girls in western wear would drive you in a convertible to the ranch house. We enjoyed our stay.

One day I drove over to Kelly Air Force Base on the other side of town to pick up some parts we needed. While I was there a big C-99 aircraft, which was a cargo version of the B-36, landed at Kelly for the first time. I think the Air Force had bought two of them. A lot of people came down to the flight line to see this plane taxi up to Base Operations. The Base Commander came in his staff car to greet the pilot who turned out to be a young 2nd Lieutenant.

It was somewhat of a surprise when another mandatory assignment came in for a teletype mechanic to go to Alaska. As short-handed as we were, Whitehead and I tossed a coin to see who would get to go. Neither of us wanted to be the one left working around the clock.

I won the toss and processed out very quickly. Wanting to go home to Canada before going to Alaska I was given a thirty day leave. While checking with Base Operations at Kelly I managed to get a "hop" on a Navy C-46 that was taking a musical group to the Marine Base at Cherry Point in North Caroline. We arrived about 6 P.M and Base Operations had no more flights going north until morning. I stayed the night with the Marine Corp crash crew and rode in their fire engine to the mess hall. The next morning I got a ride on the mail plane to Washington, D.C. and then on to a Navy Station in North Philadelphia. From there I took a train to Buffalo, N. Y. and then a bus to Toronto. After a pleasant leave I went back to Buffalo and took the train to San Francisco.

When I reached Reno a young lady got on and took the seat next to me. I found out she had been in Reno for six weeks getting a divorce and was now going back to San Francisco. She owned a candy store in San Francisco and we went out to dinner one night before I left for Alaska. I then boarded an Army Transport ship and headed north.

Blustery weather made the sea rough and Army Military transports are not the most stable of ships anyway. Lots of people were sick. The latrines and sleeping area were a mess. I stayed on deck most of the time. The dining area did not have tables and chairs. You ate standing up at a bar and had to hold your tray with one hand while you ate to keep it from sliding away. I think it took four days to get to Whittier from San Francisco.

In 1949 Alaska was still just Federal Territory. The Federal Government seemed to run everything, including the railway. Whittier to Anchorage by rail is probably about fifty miles and probably should have taken about an hour. However the engineer on this day was some kind of ardent fisherman because he stopped the train at every pond, pool or stream and tried his luck. It took us several hours to get to Elmendorf Air Force Base outside Anchorage. The base did not have any barracks space available for us new arrivals. We were loaded on two ton and a half trucks and bumped our way about two miles over very bad road to an abandoned mess hall. Electricity was still on and water. They brought out a load of steel bunks and bedding. In the morning the truck came to take us to the main base and breakfast. I was assigned to an AC&W (Aircraft, Control and Warning) squadron. I was surprised to find out the squadron already had seventeen teletype mechanics assigned and only two of these were actually working in teletype. Some of the others were working as cooks. Some were laying railroad ties and rails on a new spur on the base. Nobody seemed in a hurry to do anything with us new arrivals. Every morning we rode into the base, had roll call and were dismissed till noon. After another roll call, we were dismissed till we rode out to our so-called barracks. Mosquitoes were a real problem and I slept with a blanket over my head.

We had been at Elmendorf about five days and at noon I had wandered around to the post office on base to check if any mail had caught up with me. I overheard one of the orderly room clerks and the mail clerk talking. The mail clerk said he had heard some assignments had come in and was asking about them. The orderly room clerk told him the assignment was for a teletype mechanic to go to Ladd Air Force base in Fairbanks and he named a couple of other assignments. Slipping out of line I went around to the orderly room. Another clerk there asked me what I wanted and I told him I was supposed to be going on a new assignment to Ladd Air Force Base. He shuffled some papers and found the message covering the assignments. He gave me a form to start clearing the base. I raced around and got all the required signatures to clear the base. Orders were cut and next morning I was at base operations and got on a flight to Ladd. This was on a C138. We got a grand view of Mount McKinley as we flew north.

When we landed at Ladd Air Force Base at Fairbanks, I was met by an airman named Pruitt and after a wild ride in a three quarter ton weapons carrier arrived at my new duty squadron. This was also an AC&W squadron. The communications officer for the squadron greeted me when I got out of the truck. He told me they had lost their last teletype mechanic ten days ago and their teletype circuits were all down and would I mind going there right now and see if I could get them back in operation. I agreed and managed to get these up and running in short order, which pleased Captain Wood. He then handed me two technical manuals labeled ANTIQ-2 equipment and told me to read up on this equipment because I would have to maintain it.

Have you ever seen any old war movies where a bunch of people wearing headsets and microphones are pushing miniature planes and ships and tanks around on a table? ANTIQ-2 is a mobile version of such a set-up. Volume one of the tech manuals he gave me told how to pack it all up and load it into two one-half ton trucks. Volume two was a little more helpful.

Our squadron lived in a remote area of the base in Quonset huts. We also had a separate orderly room, dining hall building and a central latrine and washroom. The latrine was engineered for cold weather. There were two rows of seats with a large tank at one end. When the tank filled with water a counter weight would trip it and flush the two rows of seats about every ten minutes. This system was designed to prevent freezing in cold weather a favorite trick was to sit close to the tank and when it flushed you dropped a ball of burning paper into a seat and it would float under anyone sitting further down the line, causing them to leap up. Another pastime concerned a squadron detail to keep the furnace stoked with coal that heated the water for the washroom and mess hall. By really stoking this furnace it was possible to build up enough pressure in the hot water tank to blow the relief valve on top of the tank. It would go off with a big boom and send a mushroom shaped cloud of steam into the air above the building. These kind of past times seemed necessary during long cold winters.

When winter did set in newcomers to Alaska had to go through survival training course in case you came down in an aircraft. The first thing they did was take you out in a field with waist high snow and tell you to cross it. After floundering around for a while the lesson was clear. You can't travel on foot in deep snow. The next lesson was to dig a hole in the snow between two trees, run a rope between the trees to support a shelter half tent. Cover the sides of the tent with pine boughs and snow leaving a small opening in one end to crawl in. With a sleeping bag we slept the night in thirty below zero temperature. The base had a rescue team that would practice a drop over the base. Sled dogs each in his own parachute would come floating down barking all the way followed by a sled and a driver. The dogs were trained to hit the ground running so the parachute would not collapse over them and then sit down and wait to be hitched up to the sled.

Our Squadron had several radar sites scattered over the northern half of Alaska and out to St. Lawrence Island, which was only about 90 miles from the Russian mainland. In the spring of 1950 we heard of a gold strike at a place called Fishwheel on the Yukon River. A kid named Worley from Wisconsin, another guy and I rented a plane in Fairbanks so we could to up there and stake a claim. We took along five jerry cans of gas for the return trip. We flew northwest until we picked up the Yukon River and turned on it. When we found Fishwheel there was ground fog all along the river. Flying above it we could see down through it, but once you flew down into it you were blind. We noticed a mob of people running around when we would line up in an attempt to land. We gave up and headed for the weather station at Circle, to try and land. There was some snow on the ground at Circle but we needed to set down so we could refuel the plane. We came down and landed safely. The lady who ran the weather station filled us in on the happenings at Fishwheel. The whole gold strike was turning out to be a hoax. A couple of bush pilots were suspected of salting a few nuggets of gold there and creating a lot of business for them. She said all those people running around when we were trying to land, wanted to be the first ones to the plane when we touched down so they could get out of there. There were a lot of broke, hungry and desperate people. We refueled the plane and gave the gas cans to the weather people. We tramped down the snow with our feet along a path we would use for take off. We pulled the tail back against the fence at one end of the field and then started the motor and gave it the gas. At the far end of the field was a row of scrub trees and bushes. We chopped a few branches with the propeller as we barely cleared the field. We made it back to Fairbanks with no further problems.

Near our squadron area was a nice log home someone had build and probably had lost when the government developed Ladd Air Force Base. It had electricity, a big fireplace and a stove so we asked the base if we could use it as a squadron clubhouse. They agreed not knowing what we had in mind. It was not against the law to have slot machines on Federal property. We got a guy in town to put in four machines for half the take. We bought a hot dog grilling machine, soft drinks, beer and buns and other snacks we could buy at the commissary. In my hut we had a guy named Davis from Lone Wolfe, Oklahoma who played guitar and sang western songs. We got him to provide entertainment in our new club. I had used my money to get everything going. We were an instant success. We were getting people from other outfits on base coming to our little club. We were making money hand over fist. The NCO Club on Base complained to the Base Commander and we were forced to close.

Chapter 18

When the Korean War started, a reserve AC&W Squadron and a Division Headquarters in Washington State were activated and sent to Ladd Air Force Base to do the same job we had been doing with one squadron. We were all moved from our Quonset huts into new 500 man dormitories. These had large rooms, which were sub-divided by rows of wall lockers with six bunks in each alcove off a main center aisle. Lights out was a bugle call at ten o'clock. We had one character, who at the instant the bugle sounded, would flip off all the lights and then leave and take a shower. His habit of doing that upset some of us, so one night after he had turned off the lights and gone for his shower we took his bunk and put it outside. When he came back in the dark he couldn't feel his bunk and started yelling. He went back to the door to turn on the lights, but every time he went to look for his bunk we turned them off again. Still yelling he went to find the Charge of Quarters (CQ). By the time they came back we had put his bunk back where it was supposed to be. He never touched the light switches after that.

That year the Federal Government passed a law making gambling illegal on Federal territory. The bars in town and the military clubs on bases had to remove the slot machines. The only person in Fairbanks to enforce this law was the U.S. Marshal. Once a month he had to go to Juneau. During these three or four days he was away all the bars would drag the slot machines out of the back room and be back in business.

One of the people I fondly remember was Pruitt, the motor pool driver that had met me at the plane the day I arrived. His father had made a living from moonshine in Tennessee, which may have accounted for Pruitt's disdain for authority. Once while we were still in the old squadron area he had been on K.P. in the mess hall when he looked out a back window to see the Mess Sergeant putting some steak and meat cuts in the trunk of the First

Sergeant's car. He rushed out there saying "Here, let me help you with those." They, of course, were upset that he had seen them. Neither one of them hassled him after that. Some time later Pruitt was returning a vehicle to the motor pool after dark when his headlights showed someone putting gas in a civilian vehicle. He recognized the Motor Pool officer, jumped out of his truck and said "Here let me help you with that, Sir." Now he had his boss, the Motor Pool Officer under his thumb.

After we moved into the new five hundred man dormitories we would have monthly standby inspections. On inspection day everyone would be waiting in his alcoves with everything ship shape. Everyone but Pruitt. He would be lying on his bunk smoking a cigar and reading comic books. When the inspecting party arrived and the room was called to attention that was Pruitt's signal to go into action. He would leap up, shove the comic books under his mattress, and start beating the dust out of his blankets and blowing it off his shoes lined up under the bunk. The rest of us were choking back laughter and trying to keep a straight face. The inspecting party would get to Pruitt's bunk and write up his long list of transgressions and go on. The Squadron Commander eventually had had enough of Pruitt and decided to court marshal him. Pruitt had taken a Jeep into town one night and rolled it over in a snow bank. Banged up but with nothing broken Pruitt slipped back on base and reported his Jeep stolen. The night before his court marshal Pruitt slipped into the orderly room and removed every scrap of paper he could find that had his name on it. At his trial the next day the prosecution had to ask for a delay because they could not find Pruitt's records. Some time later he was court marshaled and discharged from the Air Force.

As fall turned to winter in 1950 some war games were under way. An army unit was sent up from the States through Canada using tracked vehicles we called Ducks for their transportation. When they arrived in Fairbanks they were supposed to try and penetrate the base. On the base we were issued bunches of blank ammunition and assigned defensive positions on the base perimeters. The Army "ducks" kept breaking down so they were a couple of weeks late arriving at Ladd Air Force Base. Defenders who had been firing off blank ammunition every night were now about out of ammo. When the Army did finally try to penetrate the base some idiots loaded live rounds, shooting at rocks in order to hear the shots ricochet. Army men recognize the sound of a ricochet and that ended the war games.

While I was in Alaska the Federal Government became involved in a program to supply bears to zoos around the country. One day a group of representatives from various zoos flew into Ladd Air Force Base. It was decided to send them to a radar site our unit had at Clear Alaska, about forty miles south of Fairbanks. They went down by train and were taken to the site. Bears were plentiful in the area. The radar site had a garbage dump off base where bears came to pick it over for things to eat. Lumber was brought in and cages constructed with drop doors. A can of jam would be placed in a cage and when the desired animal was close to the door, it would be pulled open with a rope. Once the bear entered, the door was dropped and secured. Lots of bears were caught and shipped. However one man insisted on trying to take a really large bear. Everyone tried to tell him that was not a good idea, but he was adamant. He selected a huge brown bear and it was duly lured into the cage and the door secured. Everyone was standing around the cage congratulating the man on his fine specimen. The bear meanwhile had finished the can of jam and headed for the door. When he realized he was trapped he let out a roar, bit through a two by four and proceeded to send pieces of lumber flying. Everyone scattered as the bear came out of what was left of the cage and ambled off.

One place I enjoyed visiting in Alaska was Arctic Circle Hot Springs. This was almost on the Arctic Circle but had hot springs coming out of the ground. Around these they had built a rustic hotel with pool and spa. In the short summer they were able to grow giant sized vegetables. Meals were served family style, and were delicious. To get there was about a two hundred mile ride from Fairbanks on a winding dirt road in a Cadillac limousine. The driver drove like a maniac but seemed to know every bump on the road. The weekend I spent there a lady and her daughter who had come south from a village named Aclavik near the mouth of the Mackenzie River where it flows into the Arctic in Canada. Her husband, I think, ran the Hudson Bay trading post there. They were nice people and I enjoyed meeting them.

Sometimes keeping the base telephone system operating was a real challenge. When we had any electrical power problems which did occur frequently, would go to our back-up power unit. However, it had been run so much and for so long a time it was beyond fixing anymore. We had been unable to get a replacement through Supply because everything was being shipped to Japan and Korea. One day Sgt. Bill Burton, who supervised the telephone cable section, came by my shop. He said he had just gotten back from Murphy Dome, which was a new military site under construction and he said there was a brand new diesel power unit just like ours sitting on the loading dock of a warehouse. Bill said that Murphy Dome would not be operational for a year, so why don't we borrow that diesel until ours comes in and then we will give them ours. Not wanting to bother any of the officers in our unit with such triviality, he and I and six of his men took some crowbars and set off for Murphy Dome in a two and a half ton truck. When we arrived we parked for a few minutes, waiting for the right moment to load it into the truck. At last no one was in sight so we backed up to the dock and using our crowbars, began inching the unit on to our truck. We had it about half way on to the truck when a civilian came out of one of the doors of the warehouse. We quickly shifted ends and pretended to be unloading the power unit. He showed no interest in what we were doing and as soon as he left we finished loading the unit and headed for Ladd Air Force Base.

Major Woods, our Communications Officer, came by the telephone plant the next morning and was surprised to see a brand new power unit installed in his telephone switching center. He asked us where it had come from and we said we thought Supply must have delivered it. A few months later some men in black suits and white shirts and ties came around looking for a power plant that had gone missing. Lots of things seem to go missing in the military. The reserve unit that had joined us from Washington State had shipped whole TIPSY-1-B radar set to Alaska. Months later it had never showed up. They traced it where it was loaded aboard ship in Seattle and they also found where it had been off loaded in

Whittier and was loaded into two boxcars. It was never seen again. If you asked me, I never trusted those people at Murphy Dome.

Once a month the Payroll Officer would have to visit the different radar sites and pay the men. One month I was able to go along as one of two payroll guards. We flew into Kotzebue first and I was surprised at their so-called runway that actually ran up hill. You landed up hill and took off down hill regardless of wind direction or velocity. From there we went on to Nome and spent the night. Nome was a pretty small town in 1950 but it did have one good eating establishment called the Bering Sea Café. It had large plate glass windows that provided an impressive view of the Bering Sea. At Nome we got on a Navy flying boat for the trip out to St. Laurence Island. From there you could see some white snow capped peaks in Siberia about ninety miles away. We were only on the Island about one hour. The people stationed there had probably the worst duty of anyone in Alaska.

There was one humorous incident concerning this place. Back at Ladd we were surprised when the Air

Force sent us a Technical Representative from RCA to work at our squadron. The only equipment we had that had any connection to RCA was some FM radio equipment, so this tech rep was assigned to S/Sgt. Hartley in radio maintenance.

The first thing he did was to take one of the transmitters apart. He was going modify it so as to improve performance. It never worked again. An irate S/Sgt. Hartley threatened to shoot him if he ever came in his shop again. Not wanting to have to ship his body back to RCA, the Squadron Commander assigned him to duty on St. Lawrence Island. He had only been there a couple of weeks when security service in Anchorage overheard a ham radio on St. Lawrence talking to someone back in the States explaining the operation of the unit and what they were doing. They should have listened to S/Sgt. Hartley. Most radio messages to and from the various radar sites was done in Morse code. T/Sgt. Capps who ran the radio shack could copy incoming Morse code while reading a book and having a conversation. One day he got a phone call from Supply saying a footlocker with his name on it had just come in.

It turned out that Capps had been in Panama for a while during World War II. When he left there in 1944 he had shipped a footlocker and now six years later it had caught up with him. When he opened the footlocker it was full of mold and decaying uniforms.

Sgt. Burton was given the task of installing a new row of telephone poles to a new building on Base. One of his trucks had an auger mounted on the back for drilling holes big enough for telephone poles. We quickly found out that the permafrost was only about a foot below the surface and was too hard to drill into. As a result we drilled the first foot in each hole and then every couple of days we could drill another foot. Climbing these poles in winter was difficult. Poles were often coated in ice and you had to use a hatchet to chop the ice as you climbed in order to be able to get your climbing hooks to bite into the pole. I was climbing a pole in this manner when my climbing hook came out. I was only up about twelve feet but I landed on frozen ground and the climbing hooks bruised my insteps. I limped around for about a month.

Chapter 19

After two years and two weeks the day came when I could leave Alaska. I had enjoyed the skiing, the fishing and the travel but it was a monastic existence where we had little opportunity to ever talk to any women. I had ordered a new blue and white 1951 Pontiac Catalina, which I intended to pick up at the factory. The dealer had shipped Alaska plates to the factory so I could drive it out of there.

I flew from Fairbanks to Great Falls, Montana and boarded a train for Chicago. About half way there we came to a sudden stop out in the country because of a derailment up ahead. Everyone had to walk across some fields carrying their luggage to where we could get on some busses. They took us past the derailment and then we boarded a new train.

In Chicago I changed trains to go to Detroit. Walking along the platform I noticed we had a club car on the train. I boarded the train, dropped my bag on a seat and made my way to the club car. I was still there when we reached Detroit. I spent the night in Detroit and caught a bus to Pontiac Michigan to pick up my new car. At the factory show room I was given the VIP treatment. After being served refreshments they brought my two-toned Pontiac Catalina with the Red Indianhead hood ornament that lit up at night.

A factory representative showed me the features on my car, shook my hand and pointed me in the direction of Canada. I had not driven in a big city for over two years so I was nervous getting through Detroit and into Windsor Ontario. After spending three weeks in Toronto I set out for Ellington Air Force Base near Galveston, Texas. The Base was not much but Galveston was a fun place. Many of the bars there called themselves private clubs. You knocked on the door, paid a dollar, was given a membership card and you gambled and partied the night away. The beaches were great and deep-sea fishing was available. The pier had a bingo hall and a dance pavilion. I felt like I was on vacation after two years in Alaska. Our Squadron Commander on the Base was a Texan from Brownsville who expected all us party animals to be at work on time in the morning. He would often pace up and down in front our barracks checking his watch and at exactly 8 A.M. he would start towards the front door. Someone inside would shout a warning and the late risers would dive out the back door as he came in the front.

After a few months in Texas I was reassigned to Enid Oklahoma. There was not much to do in the way of entertainment in Enid so I got a three-day pass at New Year's and drove back to Ellington to bring in the New Year. The weather turned bad on the return trip; rain turned to sleet and snow. In Dennison, Texas I slid sideways across a bridge but managed to straighten out on the far side. Near Ardmore, Oklahoma traffic had come to a complete stop. I was at the top of a hill behind a Greyhound bus and down below a truck had jack-knifed blocking the road. The bus driver told his passengers if they wanted to get to Oklahoma City tonight they would have to move that truck. I went with them down the hill and we were able to clear one lane. I gave the bus a head start and then followed him down the hill. We both made it down and up the other side. As I came into Oklahoma City it was still snowing heavily. A police car came up behind me and turned on his flashing lights. He asked where I had come from and how were road conditions. He said the Greyhound bus and me were the only vehicles to come in during the last two hours. I went on to Enid since I had to work the next day.

Communications maintenance varies at each Base with the particular equipment that has to be maintained. The Base Commander at Enid had a Webcor Intercom box on his desk on which he could call any of his squadron commanders at the flick of a button. Squadron Commanders thought this was a great idea so they also had Webcor units connecting to all their squadron sections. Every one of those buttons required a pair of wires to connect somewhere on the Base. Many of the telephone poles on the Base had bundles of wires on them in support of these intercom systems so people would not have to dial a telephone. About once a month we would get a call regarding a problem on the Base Commander's intercom unit. He had a florescent light in his office that would cause a hum to which he objected. He refused to believe the light was a problem. We would pretend to work on the problem until he had to step out of the office and then quickly turn off the offending light. When he returned he would compliment on how clear the unit sounded and we were good for about another month.

I was getting disgusted trying to maintain the mounting numbers of telephone wires and cables we had using a ladder and a pickup, so I ordered a telephone maintenance truck through Supply. I was sure someone would ask why we needed such an expensive vehicle and I could explain we needed it to maintain a bunch of Webcor squawk boxes, which we were not authorized. Someone would then tell us to get rid of them. I was shocked when Supply called me to pick up our new telephone vehicle.

This same Base Commander had a hang-up about officers driving expensive automobiles. He said this gave the public the impression that Air Force personnel were over paid, and he did not want Vance Air Force Base to give that impression. The parking lot a Base Headquarters quickly began to resemble a junkyard as officers left their good cars in the garage and drove an old clunker to work on the Base.

A funny incident happened one afternoon. We were installing some new phones in the Air Police building. In the squad room a group of young, recently assigned air police men were standing in formation before going on duty. The old time Chief of the section was giving them instructions before sending them out. "Tomorrow is parade day and during the last couple of parades a shaggy dog from somewhere in the housing area was a real pain in the butt barking a jumping up trying to grab the baton from the band leader. I want you guys going on patrol to pick up any dogs you see and put them in this empty room."

Off they went. After a while patrol started coming in with a mixed variety of dogs. The phone in the Chief's office was suddenly busy with calls. A red-faced Chief was answering it trying to understand what he was hearing. "Recall all patrols," he roared to the radio operator. After the last patrol had returned, the Chief strode out shouting "I told you men to pick up loose dogs not dogs in people's yards." Opening the door where the dogs were penned, he pulled one out and shouted, "Do you know whose dog this is? I don't know whose dog this is. Take all these dogs back where you found them." The next day at the parade the same shaggy dog was barking and jumping trying to get the baton from the bandleader.

I got to see my first tornado while in Enid. I was going off Base at the end of the day and on a stretch of road going into town that had a railway embankment on the east side of the road when a funnel cloud touched down in the field behind the railway embankment. Traffic was bumper to bumper and had come to a stop. The car was shaking and so was I but the funnel cloud, after a short time, lifted back up and did no serious damage.

Another incident I remember happening at Vance was a Saturday open house with lots of airplanes on display and fly over's by the different types. In Communications our job was to mount speakers on the roofs of the hangars on the flight line so the proceeding could be broadcast to the visiting crowds. These speakers were normally mounted on the base water tower and other buildings around the base. We wanted to take these down on Friday and get them relocated to the flight line. The Base Commander however said we had to wait until after retreat at 4:30 to take the speakers down. When darkness fell we had to stop but get everything working the next morning.

While at Enid I took a two-week leave and worked at a grain elevator. We would open up a boxcar and using power scoops would empty the wheat out. It was the hottest and hardest work I ever did but the pay was good.

I was pleased and surprised when I got a new assignment to a radar site on the Quantico Marine Reservation at Manassas, Virginia. We were only forty odd miles from Washington D.C. which was good in some says and bad in others. The good part was there always seemed to be things going on in Washington and lots of things to do. The bad part was that a lot of government politicians and military people in the

Pentagon would visit and require briefings. Sometimes they came by the busload. One day a group from the Pentagon came, including a General. The Controller on duty was very new and asked his senior NCO to stick close and take any questions that he could not answer. They were in the darkened radar control room and the General asked about helicopter traffic in the D.C. area. Not knowing the answer the Controller kicked at the shins of the NCO to answer. When he didn't respond he kicked at him again. "Damn it, Lieutenant, stop kicking me and tell me what coverage you have." In the darkened room the lieutenant was kicking the wrong shins.

Manassas was a really good assignment with one exception. We had a Commander who made life difficult. We began to have close order drill and marching in the afternoons. Nobody could leave the site without a pass signed by the Commander or First Sergeant. We built and painted little picket fences and installed them along walkways and around the grass in front of the barracks. Saturdays meant stand-by inspections. One day I was up a telephone pole by the main gate when an Air Force staff car drove up and stopped. Out stepped a familiar figure. Major Woods, for whom I had worked in Alaska and was now a Lieutenant Colonel and head of an I. G. Team, had come to inspect the site. Spotting me on the pole he said "Sergeant Bruno, what the hell are you doing up there?" "Trying to get up in the world, Sir?" I came down and saluted and we talked for a few minutes and then went on in to the site.

I made a point of contacting every section head and told them I knew this I. G. and if they had any problems to be sure and go see him. They all must have done exactly that because two days later our Commander was released of duty and told to go home and an assignment would follow. The next day the First Sergeant was also given a new assignment.

A week later a new Commander took over. At a squadron formation he explained his intentions to abolish a lot of the restrictions and methods of operation. While talking he noticed the white picket fences everywhere and asked how in the hell we could cut the grass, and said they would have to go. When the formation was dismissed a huge cheer went up as everyone scrambled to knock down the hated fences.

Morale shot up under the new Commander. If he had said, "Let's go take on the Marines at Quantico" the whole outfit would have gone with him. One day the Communication Officer called me in. He said the crypto equipment was down and would I take a look at it. Not wanting him to get in trouble I explained that I did not have clearance to work in crypto and was not even a citizen yet. He said he knew that but give it a try. The KLM7 crypto unit had a bunch of discs with multiple contacts. I cleaned them all and luckily it worked. I immediately went ahead and got my citizenship and continued to work on crypto when they needed me.

Tragedy struck when our Squadron Commander drowned during a weekend fishing trip. Somebody in the Air Force noted that I had worked in AntQ2 equipment in Alaska and I was alerted for shipment to the Pacific for the first hydrogen bomb test. For this assignment I would need a Q Type clearance required for atomic weaponry.

A few days later I was shocked when the Commander called me in to say I was relieved of duty until further notice because the Air Force could not find any record of a background check or any security clearance. In the meantime would I mind taking over the small Base Exchange we had. He said the Army and Air Force Exchange Headquarters were probably going to close our small branch because it was losing money. The first thing I did was fire everyone who worked in the BX with one exception, a young airman who worked for me and one I trusted. He told me about the different scams that had been going on. The first month we made a modest profit. The second month we made a huge profit from Christmas sales of watches and jewelry. The BX Headquarters wanted to know if I intended to re-enlist because they had a job for me if I did not stay in the Air Force.

In the meantime the Air Force had found my background check and security clearance, but too late for my reporting date in California, so my assignment was canceled. A short time later I received an assignment to Okinawa. To get there I flew out of Travis Air Force

Base in California to Hawaii where we stayed overnight. The mess hall at Hickam Air Force Base had divided up the dining area with a marked area for each rank. As a Tech Sergeant I was supposed to eat in the area for Techs. Instead I sat down in the S/Sgt area with a couple of S/Sgt's I had met on the plane. A large corpulent mess sergeant approached me and said if I insisted in sitting in the S/Sgt area he would arrange for me to be a S/Sgt. I told him I had lost my appetite and left without eating. This was the only Air Force mess hall where you ate by rank that I ever encountered.

From Hickam we flew on to Midway Island and then to Tokyo Japan. A few hours later we landed at Kadena Air Force Base in Okinawa. I was assigned duty in a Plan 55 Teletype switching center. Six of these centers provided worldwide links for Air Force. Engineers from Western Electric except for Okinawa supervised maintenance of these units. The man in charge here was M/Sgt Schlieder. Sgt. Schlieder had committed to memory every circuit in the center and he expected everyone in maintenance to do the same. After about a month I was able to take over one of the maintenance shifts. This was the first time I had been assigned shift work. We worked three day shifts; three evening shifts, three midnight shifts and then had three days off. A favorite pastime on our days off was to rent a motorboat with two Okinawan boatmen and visit some of the smaller islands. We would fish and snorkel and sleep on the beach.

Ancestor worship was part of the religion of Okinawa's people. The dead were placed under small stone domes called ohakas. They believed the spirit of the dead continued to roam the earth for seven years, so each year during the Oban Festival they would leave a little rice, cigarettes, messages, etc. at the ohakas. After seven years the virgin girls of the family had the unenviable task of cleaning the bones for final burial. We visited the little island of Hinzashima during Oban. We went door to door with the villagers as they sang and danced and were given food and Saki as we visited each home.

We did experience a couple of typhoons one of which was pretty strong. Our wind indicator on the Base broke at 129 miles per hour so we never knew how high it reached. One evening we were standing in line waiting for the movie theater to open and we could see a water spout out over the ocean. About fifteen minutes later it was raining hard and live fish were dropping all around.

Bob Brock, who supervised one of the other shifts and I, decided to go on leave together. We caught a hop down to Taipei Taiwan. Riding in a couple of the Pedi cabs that jammed the streets, we made it to a small hotel in the suburbs. The baths were fed from hot springs. Our room had a big fish pond in it which extended under the outside wall and into a garden. After three days we flew to Hong Kong. After checking into the hotel we went to a tailor shop we had been told about and were measured for suits. Two days later we had our suits. We went to the area called Aberdeen where they have floating seafood restaurants for an excellent dinner. From Hong Kong we took a ferry to the Portuguese colony of Macau. Chinese gun boats monitored our passage to be sure we did not stray into Chinese controlled waters. Macau had gambling arenas and a lot of gold and jade items for sale.

The next day, before boarding the ferry, we purchased a wicker hamper of live crabs to take with us.

When we got back to the hotel we painted numbers on them and held races. Afterwards the hotel staff had them cooked in the hotel kitchen. After a week in Hong Kong we headed home to Okinawa.

A new development on Okinawa was the arrival of a Marine Division, relocated from Japan. The Marines immediately took over the bars and watering holes outside the main gate of Kadina Air Base. Any Air Force people they came across were beaten to a pulp resulting in many having to be hospitalized. The base immediately retaliated and through sheer weight of numbers sent dozens of Marines to the hospital. The authorities stepped in restricting where the Marines could bar hop.

Chapter 20

My eighteen months were up so I volunteered to go to Japan. I was reassigned to Johnson Air Base near Tokyo. The flight up there was memorable. They loaded a big bulldozer on the plane, which must have maximized the load the plane could carry, because we used every foot of runway in take-off. Johnson was an interesting assignment. I worked in an underground building, which housed the Tokyo Approach Control that handled all the air traffic in the Tokyo area. A civilian named Johnny Mastich was in charge of maintenance. He was married to Japanese and had a beautiful home in the Tokyo area. Johnny had a real knack for making money. He found out that Mitsubishi was going to be giving a huge U. S. Government contract to overhaul several thousand vehicles for the Army forces in Korea. He immediately made a big investment in Mitsubishi stock. When the news became public the stock soared.

Another money-making opportunity came up when a ship loaded with cars belonging to U.S. personnel caught fire in Yokohama. They towed the ship out to open water and pumped seawater in to put out the fire. When the water was pumped out the cars were unloaded on the dock. Lloyds of London paid off on all the cars and then put them up for sale under sealed bids. Johnny saw this as an opportunity to make money so he bid on several almost new automobiles. Since regulations at the time specified that Americans could only own two cars, he placed the bids in the names of other people like me. If a bid was accepted he would pay for repairs. We would get to drive the car for a year after which time it would be sold on the Japanese market for a nice profit. The bid in my name was one of the bids accepted. A guy called Six Pack Godfrey, a couple of others and I went to Yokohama to collect the cars and register them. Registration was an all day affair so we had to stay overnight. One of the guys decided he needed some female companionship so he asked a Pedi cab driver to take him somewhere. It was a wet rainy night and with all the covers down on the Pedi cab he had no idea where they were going. The driver finally parked the Pedi cab near the top of a very steep street and after a few minutes returned with a Japanese girl. The driver said he was going to get something to eat and would be back after a while. Jones and the girl got to bouncing around in the Pedi cab and in so doing dislodged the rock the driver had placed under a wheel to keep it from moving. Gathering speed they hurled down the hill and finally crashed into a light pole demolishing the Pedi cab and threw them into the street. He was a sad sight the next day. Torn clothes, skinned up, bruised, hurting; he was a picture of a poorer and wiser man. Charley Godfrey and I had our almost new 1957 Buick towed to a Japanese garage in Tokyo. I had never seen a car completely disassembled but in two days time it was laid out on the floor and they had a list of the parts that needed to be replaced. About half the parts were available in the BX garage and the rest Johnny had shipped from the States. About a month later the car was as good as new except for the automatic transmission. We had to get it adjusted in the BX garage. For the next year Godfrey and I enjoyed having that Buick, making trips to different places.

In the 1950's stereo was big in Japan. The coffee shops of Tokyo had tried to out-do one another with different places specializing in different types of music. Whatever kind of music you liked that was a coffee shop with music to meet your taste. In going to these I met a lot of college students. They liked to mix with Americans so they could improve their English speaking skills.

With these students I went places I would never have seen. They knew where to go and how to travel cheap. The first week of July when the climbing season opened we climbed Mount Fuji. We slept at a way station about half way up, so we could see the sunrise in the morning. When we got to the top it started snowing. Down inside the volcanic cone of the mountain a building was visible where Shinto monks lived all year round. Going down the mountain was different from climbing up. We tied on woven covers over our boots and went down the mountain on the side covered with lava. Running and falling we were down in about an hour.

Godfrey and I had one real bad close call. We had been in Osaka for the World's Fair. On the drive home the road passed through a mountainous region. We had just started down around a sharp curve when we came face to face with a bus trying to pass another bus. On the side was a narrow shoulder and a sheer drop to who knows where. Somehow we managed to squeeze through without going over the edge.

Johnny Mastich had another idea. He wanted me to go into partnership with him on the purchase of this neon message sign on the Ginza. I declined because Japan had restrictions on taking money out of the country and I did not know when I would return to Japan or what I would spend any profits on.

One day we got a call telling us that the radar site on the other side of Tokyo Bay had teletype troubles and needed assistance. Another mechanic and I were dispatched to an Army helicopter unit at Misawa who would fly us over to the site. With tool kits and a spare teletype machine, we took off. Fog and clouds blanketed the mountains where the site was located and after several scary attempts to locate the site we returned to Misawa. In the meantime another team was dispatched by road to get to the site.

After eighteen months in Japan I received an assignment back to the States to Marietta, Georgia. I picked up a 1956 Pontiac in Washington, D.C. and drove up to Canada on leave. After a pleasant stay I drove down to Dobbins AFB at Marietta, GA. I was assigned to an Air Defense Division that had radar sites throughout the southeastern states. The normal routine to visit any of the radar sites was to check out a car from the Government GSA car lot in Atlanta and drive to the site. When one of the sites had teletype or crypto equipment problems someone was dispatched to help them. As I was single I got a lot of the trips.

About this time the Air Force had added German made Kleinschmidt teletype machines to the inventory. I was sent out to Cheyenne, Wyoming for a course in maintenance of this machine. On the way there I spent one night at a motel in Denver. The next morning I needed to do a left turn into morning rush hour traffic to continue my journey. Frustrated after sitting there for what seemed like forever, I finally saw a small gap in the traffic and jumped out there. Somehow I managed to squeeze in and was congratulating myself on my superior driving skills when I heard a voice saying "Blue Pontiac with Virginia plates, pull over to the curb." A few cars behind me was a police car with a loud speaker on the roof. After I pulled over I tried to tell them how long I had waited trying to get into the traffic and was just passing through on the way to Cheyenne, the policeman said "Look, we have all the idiot drivers we need right here in Denver. We don't need any idiots from Virginia. Get out of here and don't come back." I arrived at Francis E. Warren Air Force Base without further trouble.

During my stay at Francis E. Warren the only memorable incident I recall was a Saturday night visit to the State Line Bar, a Western style roadhouse near the Colorado border. A couple of classmates and I arrived there rather late in the evening. We went in and sat down at the bar and ordered some drinks. We could hear the dance music in the dancing area behind a double door. I walked over and looked through the small window in one of the doors to see how the dance looked. To my amazement a fight started at that instant. Folding chairs and beer bottles were flying through the air. The doors burst open as the struggling, screaming mass boiled out into the bar and out into the parking lot. We decided to leave and headed for our car. In the parking lot some guy with a tire iron was smashing the windows of a car. The driver jumped out, opened the trunk and was loading a shotgun. Two state police cars arrived in the nick of time to discourage any shooting. We headed back to Cheyenne. The rest of the stay at Francis E. Warren was uneventful and I returned to Marietta.

The next trip I went on was to Lake City, Florida. Heavy rains in North Florida had caused the Suwannee River to overflow and our radar site near Lake City was flooded. I was part of a team sent down there to help them become operational again. By the time we arrived the water had receded but the place was covered in mud and snakes were everywhere. We were there about a week and then returned to Dobbins Air Force Base.

About a month later our radar site at Snow Mountain in Kentucky reported crypto equipment problems. I went into Atlanta to the GSA motor pool to pick up a car to make the trip. I signed for the keys and went out to the yard looking for the matching license plate. Instead of the usual white government sedan, I had the keys to a slick looking black Ford. I opened the hood to check the oil and all I could see was chrome. I was sure someone had made a mistake and given me the wrong car. I started the engine and eased out on the clutch and the car jumped forward. I found out later that the car had been taken in a bootlegging arrest. With some spare parts and replacement crypto equipment I headed out for Kentucky. While there I got a call to go to the Marine base at Cherry Point, North Carolina where we had another radar site. Trying to go in the direction of North Carolina out of Kentucky I had to use a lot of secondary roads. On one of these roads I ran into a State Police roadblock. They were suspicious of me and the car I was driving, but let me go on through. After taking care of things at Cherry Point I returned to Georgia. I always hoped to get this same car but never saw it again.

Chapter 21

New Year's Eve 1958-59 turned out to be something special. I had dressed and left the barracks to go to the NCO Club. One of the guys from my barracks was talking to some girls in a car and called me over. The girls wanted to go to the NCO Club and wanted to know if I wanted to go along. Of course I did, and that is how I met Barbara Crane. I took her home that night. Since I was not in very good condition to drive back to the base, she decided I should sleep on the couch at her place. I woke up the next morning to find an eight-year-old girl and a boxer dog staring curiously at me. They had spent the night at her grandmother's house and were as surprised to see me as I was to see them. The eight year old was Barbara's daughter Judy and the boxer was

Bossy who probably felt he had prior rights to the couch I was on. Since Barbara Crane is now entering my story I need to talk about her life to this point. Her family came from the Commerce, Georgia area. Her father was a part-time boot-legger. He was not a good provider and Mamie, Barbara's mother, ended up moving to Atlanta with her three children, Sonny, Bobby and Barbara Ann. The family survived hard times. Sonny and Bobby went to work at an early age and would spend their years as truck drivers. Barbara was married at sixteen to Bill Hudson, also a truck driver and twelve years her senior. The marriage was not a happy one. She worked as a bookkeeper and when she became financially able, sought a divorce. She had been divorced over a year at the time we met.

By April 1959 we decided to get married. We had been married less than a year when I was notified of my impending assignment to Anderson AFB on Guam. Before reporting I had to attend a training course at Western Electric Corporation in Chattanooga, Tennessee for three weeks. In order for Judy to finish her school year it was decided I would go on to Guam and Bee

(Barbara) and Judy would follow later. I took our '56 Pontiac and drove west to Route 66. The first night on the road I kept driving until the generator failed on the car. I managed to make it into the next town and parked in front of the service door of the local Pontiac garage. I slept in the car for a couple of hours until they opened and had the generator replaced. Continuing west I had no more trouble until I reached Kingman, Arizona. I was following a truck that threw up a rock, breaking the windshield. I continued on to Bakersfield, California. I turned the car in to get the windshield replaced and went to sleep at a motel. I awoke to the noise of someone pounding on the door. It was the maid wanting to clean the room. I had slept twenty-four hours. Picking up the car, I went on to San Francisco. I turned the car in for shipment to Guam and went to Travis Air Force Base for my flight to Hawaii and on to Guam by way of Wake Island. Bee and Judy followed about two months later. Bossy, the boxer was left behind with Bee's mother Mamie.

Bee had never been out of the South, so getting to Guam was quite an experience for her. First she had to arrange the shipment of household goods with the local Army Base in Atlanta. She was supposed to ship only linens, dishes, clothes etc. as furniture was provided for the quarters on Guam. The Army insisted on shipping all our furniture and appliances. The Air Force would later try to bill me for those shipping costs. I suggested they bill the Army since it was their error. Later when we left Guam the cost of shipping everything back would again create a problem. They expected me to pay for the shipping, but I didn't have to after all was said and done.

Guam was pretty small. You could drive around the whole island in about an hour. The Navy had a nice golf course with no green fees, so golf was a popular past time. One funny incident at the golf course comes to mind. We had a new guy named Fletch who had never played golf in his life, who decided to take up the sport. He bought a set of the best clubs available, golf shoes, a fancy leather bag with covers for all his driving woods. We were waiting to tee off on the first tee, which was a temporary tee because workmen were repairing the normal first tee. Fletch was taking some practice swings on the tee and then took a mighty swipe at the golf ball, which instead of going down the fairway shot straight over to where the workmen were working on the tee, hit the truck they had parked there and rolled out at the feet of the workers. Fletch retrieved his ball, complaining about the condition of the tee and got set to try again. By this time he had everyone's attention and the workmen are edging around behind their truck waiting for his second shot. After another mighty swing it lands about twenty feet away. By this time everyone is hysterical but trying to hide it. After about twelve strokes he finishes hole number one. The second hole had a telephone cable that crossed the fairway supported by a couple of telephone poles. Fletch tees off, hits one of the telephone poles and the ball rolls back almost to where he was standing. On his next swing the impossible happens. He hit the cable crossing the fairway and the ball drops straight down. That did it. Everyone was laughing helplessly as Fletch walked over and wrapped his golf club around one of the telephone poles. He never played again.

I don't remember us having any movie theaters on Anderson Air Force Base. We watched movies out doors after dark, which was fine even when it rained. People just sat and did not care if they got wet.

Our maintenance officer Major W was a nice guy but very absent minded. I remember taking a new arrival into his office to meet him. I left them talking while I went to check on circuit outage we were working on. A few minutes later I met Major W and the new man coming down the hall. Major W said, "Sgt. Bruno I would like you to meet our new teletype maintenance man." I pretended I was meeting him for the first time much to the confusion of the newcomer.

Another newcomer was a Captain who was to be the Assistant Communications Officer. One of the first things he wanted done was to install an intercom speaker in each work center so he could monitor what was going on. This was very unpopular with the troops as they all felt he was spying on them and over hearing their phone conversations. Almost every morning the Captain would report trouble with the system and a telephone repairman would have to check the wiring and repair where the lines had been cut or disconnected. After about a month the Captain gave up trying to listen to what was going on in the work centers. The Captain had another strange habit. Outside his office door was the desk of maintenance superintendent Senior Master Sergeant Johnson. If the captain wanted to speak to Sgt. Johnson about something, he would come out of his office and slip a note into the "in" basket on Sgt. Johnson's desk, which would read "Sgt. Johnson-See me." A little irritated by this procedure Sgt. Johnson started snatching the notes out of the "in" basket as fast as they were place there and would ask the Captain, "Did you want to see me, Sir?" And this in turn would upset the Captain who would give Sgt. Johnson a specific time to come into see him.

The Commander of our Squadron was Colonel T who had some shortcomings. He knew communications but he was an alcoholic. While he was Commander the Air Force released him from duty for thirty days and put him through a drying out program. The Air Force seemed to be very tolerant of people who had a drinking problem while assigned to overseas locations. However in the States this would not be tolerated to the same degree. Colonel T at a later date would be placed in charge of an officer's club in Vietnam. (I have started using initials rather than full names where actions were not flattering. I only knew about certain circumstances where their lives touched mine.)

While on Guam I was promoted to Master Sergeant. Before our two years were up Bee became pregnant and we were anxious to return to the States before the baby was born. The day before we left for the States we were given a liquid to take to kill any parasites in our system. Bee became very sick from this and we not sure whether we should get on the plane or not but she decided to go on. She was having a miserable time and the medical people at Wake Island wanted to take her off the plane but she insisted on going on. We were happy to reach San Francisco where Bee's mother Mamie was waiting to meet us.

I had ordered a used Buick from a company in Detroit to be delivered to San Francisco. They had been unable to find one like I wanted and had shipped a 1959 Oldsmobile instead. They said to drive it to my new Base in Spokane, Washington and if I didn't like it they would send me another car. It was a nice car but I knew it was not suited for driving in snow. When we arrived in

Spokane I ordered a 1960 Chevrolet that they delivered a couple of weeks later.

Mamie had given us the sad news about our dog Bossy. The family had taken him with them to Stone Mountain Georgia. Around the top of the mountain they had a small train to take visitors around. Bossy, wearing an engineer's cap rode the train and was a big hit with everyone. Somewhere along the way he jumped off the train and slipped over the edge and fell and slid down the mountainside. The family rushed down expecting to find his body but he was still alive. He was badly skinned up and the pads of his feet were torn off. He was on television as the only living creature to survive a fall off Stone Mountain. Two months later a car killed him.

(l-r) Myself, Bee's daughter, Judy, Bee
Taken on the island of Guam (1968)

Chapter 22

My assignment in Spokane was at Geiger Field that shared runways with the local airport. We were assigned housing in a Capehart style unit in an off-base housing area. Bee was still having problems, we took her to the hospital, and she lost the baby. The day she came home from the hospital Judy and I went to the local pound to get a new dog. On the lawn outside the pound was a black and brown puppy attached to a rope you would normally use to tie up an ocean liner. We petted the pup and went on into the pound. We looked over all the dogs they had but nothing compared to the puppy we had seen outside. We named him Shorty because he had short legs and a long body. We always said he was a dog and a half long and a half a dog high. Our base housing unit had no fences so Shorty had to be tied to the clothesline when he was outside. He became very popular with the children in the neighborhood. The base commander's daughter would untie Shorty and take him home with her but we always knew where to find him.

Mamie stayed about two months and took the bus back to Atlanta. Judy took up horseback riding and wanted us to buy a horse. We could not afford one so we had to disappoint her.

I did not like our Chevrolet. At highway speeds the fins in the back would lift the back end up and made you feel you were losing control of the steering. We sold the car and bought a 1957 Cadillac from a Major on the base. To try it out we made a trip to Seattle for the weekend. I had to add oil every time we stopped for gas. I had made a bad mistake buying that Cadillac. To add to our troubles, we found out when we got back to Spokane, that someone had broken into our post office box and my paycheck was missing. The agents sent to investigate gave the impression that they thought I was involved in some way. I was very upset with their line of questioning. About a week later they called me in again and told me that the check had been cashed at a store in Spokane and wanted to know when the last time I had been in that store. I told them I did not know where the store was but they made me write my name about twenty times so they could compare it with the endorsement on the check. They finally decided I had not signed the check and they went after the store owner for cashing the check without proper identification.

We had been in Spokane about ten months when we got word Geiger Field was closing. People began shipping out going in all directions. The base commander, Col. Johnson, was promoted to Brig. Gen. and assigned as the Air Attaché in the American Embassy in Oslo Norway.

I was going to Otis Air Force Base on Cape Cod, Massachusetts and would be working on the Texas towers, which were radar units out in the Atlantic. Bee took our Cadillac into a dealer to see if it could be repaired. She asked the mechanic if he thought the car would make it to Cape Cod and he said he didn't think it would make it to the city limits of Spokane. She then tried to make a deal on a 1959 Pontiac wagon. She and the salesman were fifty dollars apart on the price. She told him how poor she was and fifty dollars would not mean much to Mr. Utter, the owner, and that after all you can't take it with you. The salesman said, "You don't know Mr. Utter." If he can't take it with him, he ain't going. She gave them the fifty dollars.

We bought a tent and other camping gear to use going across country. Near the end of May 1963 we left Spokane and made it into Yellowstone National Park. I set up the tent and we managed to cook up a meal. During the night water froze in the tent. Bee, a Southern Belle, was not happy about that and insisted we pack up and leave. After having breakfast and seeing "Old Faithful" we started out. While still in the park we had to come to a stop because of some bears. I was waiting for the bear, in front of the car, to get out of the way when Shorty, our dog, let out a snarl. Judy had opened one of the back door windows and Shorty was eyeball to eyeball with another bear. Fortunately the bear backed off.

Around noon we had reached Gray Bull Wyoming. Going through town I realized I had missed a turn and had to double back on a side street. Coming up to an intersection I hit a big bump on the road and hit the brakes at the same time. The roof rack, loaded with camping gear, broke loose, shot over the front of the car and out into the intersection. There was a garage in the next block so they had their wrecker lift everything to their yard. I bought some new straps and suction cups and we were soon on our way. We drove until we reached Mount Rushmore and spent the night. When we reached Minneapolis we got a motel so we could shower and clean up. The next day we took a ferry across Lake Michigan to the Michigan side and drove through to Toronto.

Two weeks later we arrived at Otis Air Force Base on Cape Cod in Massachusetts. While we were in route, the Air Force had closed down the Texas Towers, but had been unable to switch my assignment. We rented a big Cape Cod style home in the village of Catamet. The owner was Major White, a member of The Strategic Air Command (SAC), Inspector General (IG) team. His teen-age son John was living in the house and stayed on with us after we moved in. He was our guide on where to go and what to do in Cape Cod.

Bee took Judy to Atlanta to see the family. Judy decided she wanted to stay in Atlanta with her father and go to school there. We agreed and Bee came on home. The first cool month of fall brought a shocking increase in our utility bills. We found a Captain to take over our lease and moved on Base. Since I was excess to personnel needs I got a lot of odd jobs to do such as running the United Fund drive etc. The Base sent me and two other NCOs' to California to attend the Air Defense Command senior NCO school. To save travel funds they decided we should go to California by military aircraft. We boarded an old C-47 twin-engine aircraft and flew up to Selfridge Field in Michigan to pick up some more people. We flew to Virginia and down to Missouri. After three days of travel we finally arrived in California.

Six weeks later we were ready to go home. Base transportation did not know we were supposed to wait for an aircraft to come get us, so they booked us on a midnight flight into Boston. We were in the first class section and the only other passenger in first class was the head of the Greek Orthodox Church. His assistant priest had to ride in the tourist class section. The Base was upset with us for traveling commercial but we played innocent and said Base transportation in California was the ones who sent us commercial. We heard later that it took a week for the others to get back home.

President Kennedy and all the Kennedy clan traveling between Washington and Hyannisport used Otis Air Force Base. It was not unusual to walk into the NCO Club and find a dozen Kennedy children running around and harried Secret Service agents trying to keep track of them. When President Kennedy was killed this Base really went into shock. The Base would never be the same.

I was very excited to learn I was going to Oslo Norway on my next assignment. A week later it was canceled and I was very disappointed. A week later I was again notified I was going. Personnel Section then told me they thought it was canceled again. Mystified and upset I found out that another NCO somewhere was trying to get the assignment and had political pull or something. Air Force finally confirmed I was going. Bee went back to Atlanta one more time to see her mother, who now had cancer, and to bring Judy back. We put our station wagon in storage at a small garage and shipped out to Norway.

While we were waiting for our sponsor to get to the airport, I called General Johnson at the American Embassy and told him where we were. He immediately came down to the airport to see us. He was wearing an old sweater and did not look like a General.

We had rooms at a place called the Baptist Seminary where we stayed until our furniture arrived and we could rent somewhere to live.

It took about a month, but we found a new home for rent. The owner who worked for Norsk Hydro Electric Company was being sent to school in France. The school was the equivalent of our Harvard Business School. We would be able to have the place for a year. Shorty, our dog, had been in quarantine since we landed, but the authorities said we could bring him home if we had a double walled pen he could be kept in when he was not in the house. The quarantine was to last for six months and they were very strict on this. I immediately started constructing a large walk-in pen in our yard. This aroused the curiosity of our neighbors who wanted to know what I was making. I explained it was for our dog that was in quarantine. They discussed this information among themselves and they decided this must be a very valuable dog and wanted to know how much he had cost. I told them ten dollars, which really perplexed them. After our pen had been duly inspected and approved, we brought Shorty home. In the six weeks he had been in quarantine he had lost his voice from barking all that time. We had previously taught Shorty to sort of sing along with us on a couple of songs but he could not do it now. When I first put him in his new pen the neighbors gathered to look at him. They wanted to know what kind of dog he was and I said he was a mixed breed. That information started them laughing. In Norway I found out any mixed breeds that were born were immediately put to death.

My new job was with NATO. We had a mixed group of Allied personnel from Denmark, Norway, Britain and American Navy, Air Force and Army. This was a great assignment. We were off on the National holidays of Norway, Britain and our own American holidays. During the winter we had every Wednesday afternoon off to go skiing. We bought skis for all the family. Judy and Bee took ski lessons and soon got the hang of it.

Our Base was an underground complex at a place called Kolsas. Going to work was a mile walk past blast proof doors and down long tunnels. The Base had originally been dug out of the mountain during the German occupation of Norway. The Norwegian people had long memories about that occupation and the fact that Sweden had allowed passage of German troops through their territory. NATO stationed no Germans in Norway but some General Staff were allowed in during training exercises. NATO was using Dutch and Norwegians made cryptographic equipment so I was sent down to Holland for a fifteen-day course to learn their system. Our headquarters at Kolsas had operational bases under its command in Norway, Denmark and Northern Germany, so I got to do some more traveling.

Bee's cousin, Barbara Jean and her husband Harold, who worked at the Embassy, were living in Stockholm Sweden so we made a trip to see them. In the 1960's Swedish cars were still driving on the left so that was a little tricky. We had brought a 1500- series Volkswagen and I managed to make no mistakes while driving in Sweden for a whole week. On returning to Oslo I turned on to the road going to Fornibu Airport on the wrong side of the road, but managed to escape unscathed. Barbara Jean and family had the same problem when they came to Norway to visit us.

While I was a prisoner of war in Germany I had known a Norwegian by the name of Paul Mulvik. He had been captured on the island of Spitsbergen North of Norway. Prisoners taken there were marched down the length of Norway and then shipped to Germany. Previous to that he had been a volunteer helping the Finns in their war with Russia and had earned the Mannerheim medal. As the Russians started getting close to our camp Mulvik had worried that the Russians might have some knowledge of his background. Near the end of the war he escaped from our camp and made his way up to the Baltic coast, slipped aboard a Swedish ship and got back to Norway. I found his name in the Oslo telephone directory and gave him a call. He invited me to his home. He was now a Captain in the Army. I was shocked when he pretended not to remember me since we had spent a lot of time together. I never contacted him again.

NATO had a couple of cottages, or huts as they called them, in Norway that we could sign up for and use. We had signed up to use one of these, which was on a rather big lake. Two other couples came with us and Judy had also brought along one of the girls in her class at school, the daughter of Major Theopilus. The Major and his wife were having problems and the daughter stayed with us occasionally to get away from home. The first morning we woke up to cold windy weather with white caps on the lake. We stayed inside and played cards. The girls were bored and wanted to go out in the rowboat. We told them no way, it was too windy. So they went outside and sat in the boat where it was tied to the dock. We had been playing cards for a while when I glanced outside and realized there was no sign of the girls or the boat. We rushed out to the dock but there was no sign of them. In a panic we jumped in the car and raced down the road paralleling the lake trying to spot them. We rounded a corner and here came the two girls walking home. Their story was that they had seen two Norwegian boys in a boat and decided to go talk to them. They quickly realized their mistake. Unable to get back to the dock they did manage to beach the boat. I was very upset with the girls but so grateful they had come to no harm. They escaped with a tongue-lashing.

We really enjoyed Norway. After the first year we moved into a ground floor apartment where we became acquainted with some of the other tenants. The Americans assigned to Kolsas hosted a Christmas party every year for all the orphans in the Oslo area. These kids lived in neighborhood homes with adult supervision and attended regular schools. One year I got to run the show and it was a great experience.

The Norwegian Army held a ski and shoot competition every year. Of course the Norwegians dominated this affair but we other nationalities were expected to compete. This was a timed event. First you skied to a firing range and got a score for shooting. Then you skied through an area and on a map you showed any tanks, trucks or people you observed. Then you came to a building where you tried to toss dummy hand grenades at an open window. Then you skied on to the finish line.

I found out I was not very good at any of that stuff and got a low score.

Before leaving Norway I was promoted to Senior Master Sergeant.

When we left Norway we flew to Scotland and stayed for a week. At the airport I rented a car and drove to Edinborough. Driving on the left was a little easier since I had a left hand drive type car. Then we drove up to Huntly and Bee and Judy got to meet my aunt Georgina. We then went up to Loch Ness and back by way of Loch Lomond to Glasgow. We then departed for the States.

Chapter 23

At Idlewild airport in New York we rented another car and headed out. I got lost almost immediately. Seeing three guys standing on the street, I stopped and asked directions to the Connecticut Turnpike. All three of them had different ideas of how to get there and I thought they were going to get into a fight over what was right. We said "Thanks" and drove off none the wiser. Fortunately we did saw a sign for the turnpike.

In Connecticut we picked up Shorty, our dog, who had flown straight back to the States from Norway, so he was glad to see us. On Cape Cod we got our station wagon back with new tires, hoses and belts. It was ready to go. From there we drove up to Canada to see the family. After a week we drove to Atlanta. Judy did not want to stay in Atlanta this time but came on to Jacksonville Arkansas to my new Base.

My assignment to here had been as a Master Sergeant. Now that I had been promoted to Senior I had too much rank for the job. This was a Strategic Air Command Base with a missile and a bomb wing. The choice I was given was to "on the job" train into airborne radio maintenance or be a First Sergeant for a squadron. Not liking the idea of on the job training into such a high tech skill as radio maintenance, I chose to become a First Sergeant for a year. I was assigned to the Fourth Munitions Maintenance Squadron as their First Sergeant.

Morale in the squadron was rock bottom and it took me a little while to find out why everyone was giving me the cold shoulder. The previous First Sergeant had a bad track record. On Fridays he would go around the barracks and rub grease on the shower walls and then hold a standby inspection on Saturday. He restricted one NCO to base then went into town and tried to make out with his wife. On top of this, weapons maintenance personnel were going to Vietnam as fast as their year was up in the States. The first thing I did was to do away with the Saturday barracks inspection. As long as they kept things tidy, there would be no inspections. That got me in good with the people in the barracks right away.

Then another problem developed. Someone stole the television set in the day room of the barracks. The Charge of Quarters (CQ) had made his rounds at midnight and the TV was there. At 1:00 A.M. he made his rounds and the TV was gone. He reported the theft immediately. The Base recreation fund was reluctant to replace the TV saying we were careless in protecting the property. I disagreed and went to the next fund meeting. The members all appeared to be Colonels. They began discussing a new courtyard they wanted to build onto the base golf course club house. The cost was going to be about $128,000 and they didn't see why it couldn't be done. Before the meeting I was already put out by the golf course people. Each squadron was assigned one hole, which they were supposed to police up once a week and pick up any trash. I had never found anyone in the squadron that played golf, so I never bothered sending anyone out to clean it up. Now and again I would get a call telling me there were some papers on the tenth hole. I would apologize and tell them we would take care of it the next turn we were out there. Not being able to contain myself any longer I asked to speak. I told the committee that we had been without a television in our dayroom for a month, through no fault of our own, and that as far as I knew no one in the squadron played golf and I personally could not see how they could spend that much money on the golf club house, but could not replace a stolen television for the barracks, and asked them to reconsider our request for a TV. I got the TV along with a lot of cold stares from some of the people in the meeting. During the year I was First Sergeant we never sent anyone out to the golf course.

One day I got a call from Base Personnel to come down to their office. They told me they were changing my primary job classification from Communications Maintenance Superintendent to First Sergeant. I said I wanted to stay in communications but they would check with SAC. Worried about what SAC would do and not wanting to stay as First Sergeant, I took a three-day pass and caught a hop to Texas. Landing at Bergstrom AFB I lucked out. A couple of trainer planes from Randolph AFB, where I wanted to go, were doing some practice landings at Bergstrom. The tower called one of them and asked if they would take a passenger back to Randolph when they were finished. That same afternoon I was able to walk into Air Force Personnel Headquarters. I located the section handling my AFSC and told them my story. I apologized for coming there but had no where else to turn. After listening to my story the personnel expert checked the computer to see what was going on. To his surprise he found out that SAC was not even reporting me as being assigned to Little Rock Air Force Base. He said, "I know a WAF Colonel in the Pentagon that will love to twist SAC's tail with this one." I told him I did not want to make waves; I just wanted to stay in communications. He flagged my personnel file and told me to go back to Little Rock because anything SAC tried to do has to come to him for approval, which was not going to happen. I thanked him and managed to make my way back to Little Rock Air Force Base. A few days later I got another call to come to Base Personnel. Once again they had the papers for me to sign and again I refused. The personnel officer was brought in. He said he had personally talked to SAC and whether I signed or not SAC was going to make me a First Sergeant and that I was dismissed. Next day I got a call from Randolph saying SAC had finally reported my presence at Little Rock. Air Force sent a message to everyone concerned saying assignment to Vandenberg AFB was disapproved, change of primary AFC was disapproved, and an assignment for me would follow.

I was expecting to go to Vietnam but instead an assignment to Taipei Air Station on Taiwan and this was an accompanied assignment. I could take the family along. We bought a four door black Ford to take to Taiwan. I left our Pontiac wagon with Bill Burton (Alaskan buddy) who put it in an old barn. After a leave in Atlanta we drove to Seattle and turned our Ford in for shipment to Taiwan. We flew by way of Alaska and Japan to Taipei. We checked into a Chinese hotel while waiting for our furniture to arrive. Shorty, our dog, was left in Atlanta with a friend because dogs had a habit of disappearing in Taiwan. Mongolian barbecue, a popular dish in Taipei, often contained meat of questionable origin. We rented an upstairs unit in a four-plex building. The owner lived in a hut behind our place. He said if he showed any sign of wealth or opulence the government would immediately level a tax on him so he had to appear to be poor.

I went to work at Taipei Air Station. We had an AFSC Communications Division Headquarters there and a squadron at CCK Air Base and another in Tainan at the south end of Taiwan. The easy way to travel down island was by rail, which was fast and efficient. On one occasion I had the opportunity to fly back to Taipei on a Chinese Air Force C-47. When we boarded I found out there was a bunch of Chinese women and children dependants with a couple of crates of chickens going along. We flew in solid clouds and they had no radar on a C-47. When we reached Taipei air space the pilot called in for landing instructions. Chinese military had priority over international airlines or anybody else so the controllers had to juggle them around and land us first. When I got into the terminal I got on an escalator and here comes a guy jumping and knocking people about as he comes down the up escalator. When I reached the next floor I saw the movie cameras. I never did know the movie I was in and the Oscars never called.

Bee got an ear infection and the local hospital decided to air evacuate her to Japan to see if they could correct the problem. They said they could not and she would have to go back to the States for an operation. In the meantime Judy had graduated from High School and wanted to return to the States and live with her father and attend dental hygienist college. Bee left for Denver where she could be examined and be treated at Fitzsimmons Army Hospital.

In the meantime as my time left was short, Air Force assigned me as close to Fitzsimmons as they could which was in Cheyenne Wyoming.

I sold our Ford, shipped the furniture and flew into Memphis Tennessee where Bill Burton met me. We then went back to his place and I picked up our old Pontiac wagon and headed for Denver.

Bee had the operation, which was a success and restored the hearing in that ear.

We checked with Base Housing Office at Warren Air Force Base but the only unit they had was a tiny two bedroom. After getting permission to live off base we decided to go house hunting. We left Denver in a driving snowstorm and made it into Cheyenne. The realtor showed us two houses and we bought the second one we looked at. It was a 3-bedroom tri-level out in an area called Buffalo Ridge.

I was back in SAC. This was a missile support base with Atlas missiles in silos around Wyoming and surrounding states. My new job was keeping tabs on all our communication systems and the status of individual equipment pieces. We had a Commander's briefing every morning so I always came in early so as to have the answers for any outages that were still waiting to be fixed. Crews were dispatched by truck to repair or replace equipment. It was a busy job but I enjoyed it.

On the home front Bee and I got a call from Judy in Atlanta that she was pregnant. The father of the baby was identified as being Tony Waters. She had met him in the hospital in Taipei while she and I were visiting Bee. They had kept in touch and he had visited her in Atlanta. He was 29 years old and in the process of divorcing his third wife and Judy was eighteen. They were married and took up residence in a mobile home in Muleshoe Texas. When our grandson Manning was born we visited them in Muleshoe.

Back in Cheyenne Bee found a great deal on a car - a German made Opal, which we bought. We had the car a week and I had gone to the Commissary and was driving home after work. I was sitting at a red light, the third car back, when a lady in a Buick with no brakes smashed into me and knocked me into the car in front of me and knocking that car into the first car. The force of the blow ripped the bolts out that were holding my seat to the floor and jammed my knees into the dashboard and gave me a severe whiplash. The Opal was totaled. I hurt for a month but nothing was broken. After that experience, I felt much safer driving my Pontiac wagon, which was built like a tank.

After a long hard Wyoming winter I was ready for some fishing. Chief Wetzel, Senior Master Sergeant Jack (I forget his last name) and I checked out a boat and motor from Special Services. Our plan was to fish on the North Platte River. We checked with the Game and Fish Department on the conditions on the river and was told that it was fine. Weather was overcast and cold so we were wearing parkas and combat boots. None of us had been on the river before but did not anticipate any problems. We took two cars. When we got to the river we were surprised to see the water was still brown from the Spring run-off. We unloaded the boat and hid it in some bushes and then drove down river to a town called Saratoga. There we left one car and the boat trailer and went back to the boat in the other car. We had flotation cushions to use rather than life vests. I sat in the back and ran the motor while Wetzel and Jack put out lines. The river was flowing so fast we did not need the motor so I turned it off and just steered with a paddle. There was no way we were going to catch any fish. The water was so murky the fish could never see our bait. But we were committed and had to go on down stream to Saratoga. The river made a sharp bend and there were three channels we could now enter. Not being able to see any problem I steered for the middle one. On the shoulders of the islands were mounds of driftwood. Suddenly I spied a large log about the size of a telephone pole sticking out into the channel. I shouted at Wetzel and Jack who were facing the back to paddle. They looked around, saw the log and started to paddle. We almost made it but the log tipped the boat off and we were all in the water. I grabbed hold of some driftwood and was able to climb up on to the island. Jack was doing the same further down the channel. Wetzel was caught under the driftwood and could not move but his head and one arm was above the water. I took off my parka and Jack and I climbed back down breaking and kicking driftwood until we could get hold of Wetzel. Between the two of us we managed to pull him up on top of the driftwood and on to the island. We were cold, wet and still in trouble. We could see a ranch house and some buildings about a half a mile away. We shouted but could see no sign of life around the buildings. We talked about one of us trying to swim to shore but the water was so cold we didn't like the chances of making it. Just then we spotted a young boy at the ranch house bouncing a ball against the wall of a building. We started yelling at him and he looked around. We waved at him and he waved back and began bouncing the ball again. We yelled in unison and this time when he looked around we motioned for him to come down to the river. When he got close we shouted and asked if anyone was at the ranch. He said no that his folks had gone into Saratoga to shop. We asked if they had a phone and he said they did. We told him to call the sheriff's office in Saratoga and tell them we need someone to get us off the island. He trotted away to the ranch house. Within the hour a pick-up truck towing a boat and trailer came past the ranch house and down to the river. Three young guys backed the trailer to the river unloaded the boat and started a big motor. We were off the island and on our way to Saratoga to pick up our vehicle. We thanked our rescuers and retrieved our other vehicle and went home.

The base considered making us pay for the boat and motor but could not prove we were careless so they let the insurance pay for them.

An on going research program in the Air Force was missile defense. Not much progress had been made but another test was scheduled. SAC would launch an atlas missile from Vandenberg Air Force Base in California and another interceptor missile would be launched from an island in the South Pacific. I don't know how they selected people but I was part of a group sent to Vandenberg to observe the launch. I had never seen a missile launch except on film so I was looking forward to it. We flew into LAX where we were to change to a small feeder airline called Pacific Airlines. We watched respectfully as two very muscular women loaded our baggage on to the plane. It turned out that two women were also the flight attendants on our flight into Lompoc, California. The next morning we had a briefing and then were dismissed to await the launch that afternoon. Somebody told us the bowling alley served a good lunch so we took off looking for it. When we went in I heard a scream and a familiar figure came running over. It was SMSgt Boldizano's wife who had been in Norway with us. I introduced her to the guys I was with and she proceeded to update me on people we knew in Norway. General Johnson had retired. One of his sons had gone to the Air Force Academy. He had been making a little extra money selling hot dogs. Unfortunately the mustard container he was using had come from a mess hall, so he was dismissed for misuse of Government property. He was out of the Air Force and now flying cargo for Tiger Airlines on Taiwan. While she talked the other guys had managed to eat lunch and were ready to go. I missed lunch but did get to watch the Atlas thunder into the sky. A successful launch, but the intercept missed. We headed for the airport and Cheyenne.

Trouble on the home front. Judy had caught Tony Waters messing with one of his female students. He was working as an Athletic instructor in the local high school. When Judy sued for divorce the girl's parents opted for a marriage rather than the scandal of putting him in jail. Bee and I were happy he was out of the family.

Driving to work early in the morning I would encounter very little traffic. On the way to the base I would use the freeway for about three miles. Sometimes I would floorboard my Pontiac wagon just to blow the carbon build up out of the engine. On this particular morning I was doing just that. There was one pick-up truck on the road and I had just passed him and was about to go under an overpass when a deer bounded out and froze in my headlights. I could not switch lanes because that pick-up truck was there somewhere and all I could do was jam on the brakes. I hit the deer, which literally exploded smearing the windshield where I could not see a thing. The wagon went into a skid and bounced over the center dividing median and came to a stop on the other side of the freeway. I pulled off on the shoulder counting my blessings. The guy in the pick-up had stopped, loaded the deer in the back of his truck and drove off. All I had to replace on the wagon was one bent rim and a plastic screw that adjusted one of the headlights.

Cheyenne apparently was a dangerous place to live, so when my new assignment to Vietnam came in I was ready to go. We put our house on the market but when it was time for me to depart it had still not sold, so Bee stayed in Cheyenne for another month at which time it sold.

Chapter 24

I flew out of Travis Air Force Base in San Francisco to Cam Ran Bay Vietnam. The next day I flew on to Pleiku. This was a base we were trying to turn over to the Vietnamese. The VNAF or air force was trying to maintain the telephone plant and the ARVN or army people were trying to maintain the telephone cable system. If the ARVN needed some helicopter support from the VNAF they may or may not get it. The ARVN guards around the base were just as likely to sleep rather than guard. Twice the Viet Cong walked right in and rocketed the control tower.

The hut where I stayed had sixteen rooms with a central washroom and screened in porch. About a four-foot rock wall ran along outside the walkway to our rooms, which offered protection from any close hits. All weapons were supposed to be locked up until an attack, so as to keep people from shooting one another. But everyone had some kind of weapon hidden away.

We had some crazy people living in our hut. They would be playing cards in our screened in porch, when there would be an explosion somewhere. Someone would say, "What's that noise?" On the next bang someone would say, "That's outgoing." When the next round would go off a lot closer, they would decide that was "Incoming." They would rush and get their tape recorders and record a running commentary on the firing to impress the folks back home. Our best defense was two dogs that lived in our hut at night and went to work with us in the daytime. Their names were Beggar Wolf, a big brown male and a smaller female named Peanuts. If they started barking at night you paid attention. We could tell the way they barked if it was a rat they were after, a snake or someone was moving in the area.

When I first arrived, Peanuts had just had a litter of pups and had them in the bomb shelter in our area. The new commander of the Americans at Pleiku decided to inspect the bomb shelters. Halfway down the darkened stairs of the shelter he was met with a vicious snarl and two eyes gleaming in the dark. He ordered the dog be shot but the Air Police knew whose dog it was and told us to get her out of there, which we did.

Snakes were common, and sometimes a problem, especially cobras. I was coming out of the door of the telephone exchange talking to the guy behind me when I heard the door slam. I glanced back to find I was alone and a cobra was crossing the sidewalk behind me. The other guy had seen the snake and jumped back inside and slammed the door.

Another snake incident was sort of funny but not to the person involved. We got a new First Sergeant in who was an early riser. He started out going to the office alone in the morning. This particular morning he decided to use the bathroom. He went in and sat down in an open door stall. As he did a cobra rose up under the sink in front of him. He froze staying perfectly still and the snake finally lay back down. To get out of there he had to take two steps toward the snake, pulling up his trousers as he went. He tore the door to the washroom right off its hinge as he left. The Air Police came and shot the snake. The next morning they killed another cobra right outside the building. It seems cobras have the ability to track their mates, so if you kill one be prepared for another one to show up.

We had a small group of Montagnards, a mountain tribe that had a temporary camp nearby. Our Communication Squadron befriended this group. We would take their hand-made blowguns, bows and arrows to Saigon and sell them to the headquarter types there who wanted trophies to take home. With the proceeds we had purchased a rice-processing machine. This machine made a huge difference in the amount of rice they could use to feed themselves or to make rice wine. With a few chickens, goats and pigs they could move at a moments notice to safer ground. They were happy to help the Americans to kill Vietnamese, who abused them as far back as they could remember. One baby-faced teenager was already credited with fifty Vietnamese deaths.

I had been in the country a little over two months when I got a message from the Red Cross that my mother was dying of cancer. I was given an emergency leave and flew back to Toronto. She passed away the same day I arrived. After the burial I took my sister Myrtle to Kansas with me where Bee had ended up. After selling our house in Cheyenne, she had gone to Florida, rented an apartment for a month. She had a scare from an intruder. Shorty, our dog made him beat a hasty retreat. The Air Force had set up a base in Kansas as a waiting wives base for families whose husbands were overseas or missing in action. I spent a week there and headed back to Vietnam. I got there the same week we got a new Squadron Commander. He was holding his first Commander's call in the Base Chapel, when the rockets started coming in. Lots of noise but not much damage.

One of the main duties our squadron performed was to maintain and operate a TACAN unit at a place called Dakto, up near the tri border area of Vietnam. To get there by road from Pleiku to Kontoun, which had had a French garrison before Vietnam threw the French out. That was the last American base. Dakto was a Vietnamese ARVN base with only two American advisors, when they were not out in the bush somewhere. We had six people assigned there living on the base in a house trailer dug into a hole in the ground. They maintained the TACAN and the power unit needed to keep it running. The TACAN provided instant position information to any American planes in the area. No one liked to fly that area if the TACAN was not functioning. For the ARVN Dakto was like their "F" troop. If one of them got in trouble he would get assigned to Dakto. Our people were always nervous about what would happen if the Viet Cong made a serious attack. One night they did try to over run the Base but the ARVN fought like tigers and killed about forty attackers. They knew if they did not, they would end up as porters carrying packs on the Ho Chi Min Trail.

About two or three times a week a pick-up truck from our squadron would make that run to Dakto. We always tried to make it up and back the same day. One afternoon we got a call they needed a part and rather than drive and stay overnight we got a ride on a chopper to take myself and another Sergeant up there. While on the way the chopper got a call about a firefight and could they help. The pilot said he could and changed directions. Another call and someone said they did not need them, so we went on to Dakto.

An additional problem was fuel for the power unit. They had a small fifty-gallon trailer and they would run down the road to Kantoun almost every day. To solve that problem another Sergeant and I went to the motor pool in Pleiku to see if we could get a tanker truck. We walked into the office in the motor pool and told the Army Sergeant our problem. He told us that Air Force people needed to go through channels if we needed a vehicle and at the same time he was slipping us a set of keys with vehicle numbers on a tag. We found the truck and drove it to the fuel dump. They did not want to give us any fuel, but finally relented. We took it to Dakto and the ARVN dug a hole next to the power generator to park it in. I had been in Vietnam about seven months when our unit was deactivated and communications at Pleiku was turned over to the Vietnamese. I was reassigned to a communications installation and engineering unit at Korat in Thailand.

My new job was what they called a circuit rider and involved a lot of travel. Anywhere new communication equipment was being installed in Thailand or Vietnam, I had to make a monthly visit and see if we were on schedule or if there were problems either equipment or personnel that needed attention. A week after I left Vietnam I was back in Danang.

One of my favorite places to visit was the town of Chang Mei, because it was in the mountains, it was cooler than lower areas of Thailand. The Air Force was installing a large satellite communication complex about twenty miles from Chang Mei. The area around this new complex was controlled by strong groups of bandits who were busy growing poppies and selling opium. They left us alone not wanting the Thai army to interfere with their drug trade. We stayed off those roads after dark. The King of Thailand had a summer palace in Chang Mei so we installed an Instrument Landing System at the Air Port so the King's plane could safely operate and land in poor visibility conditions.

Driving in Thailand was always a thrill since they drive on the left. When I had to go to Vietnam I would either drive or take a bus to Bangkok since there were regular flights out of there. The bus driver would usually stop and buy a Buddhist protective item that he would hang over the visor. With this he was safe for the day, even if he drove like a maniac. A lot of the passengers, like myself, did not share that safe feeling.

I got to make a quick trip back to Wheeler AFB in Hawaii for a conference. I did make one trip back to Pleiku. I found out our dog Beggar Wolf had died from eating a rat that had eaten some poison. Peanuts had new people taking care of her and would have nothing to do with me.

At Christmas I was able to get an R & R back to Hawaii where Bee met me. We managed to go to the Don Ho show before we both came down with the flu. I got Bee to her return flight and went back to Thailand.

Finally, my time to return to the States came. I did not have to worry about a replacement because my job was changed to someone of Major rank. Since we had a Major available to do the job, I took him around all our job sites before leaving.

Chapter 25

My new assignment was at Lowry Air Force Base at Aurora, Colorado on the outskirts of Denver. My job was maintenance superintendant of the Communications Squadron. I was promoted to Chief while in this job.

One of the missions of this Base was a drug rehabilitation program. Instead of just discharging drug users, the Air Force decided to try treating them and keeping them in the Air Force. Some of these patients worked part time in normal jobs on the Base. I had several telephone maintenance people in this category. They worked well for some time until we discovered they had cut a hole in the floor of the chapel leading from the crawl space to where the wine for the sacrament was stored. Another man appeared to have achieved a religious conversion until it was discovered he had a stash of drugs in the choir loft.

We lived in quarters on the base. Judy had decided to go to college so we took her son Manning to live with us rather than have him in day care every day. Judy was enrolled in Midwestern University in Wichita Falls, Texas. The owner of the house she and a girl friend had rented decided to sell the house, so Bee and I bought it so she would have a place to live. Bee had finally sold our Pontiac wagon so we now had a pick-up truck and a small Ford car. About once a month we would make a run to Wichita Falls with a load of groceries, clothing, etc. These visits also helped Manning to stay in touch with his mother.

Our Commander asked me to sponsor the new maintenance officer coming from Taiwan. I was happy to do so especially when I found out it was Captain Leroy Foust, who had been at Cheyenne, Wyoming during our time there. Base housing owed me some favors for up grading their telephone system, so I was able to secure a set of quarters for Leroy that would normally have been assigned to a Colonel. He, of course, was delighted.

Once again I received an over seas assignment. This time to Kwang Ju in South Korea. We bought the house next door to Judy in Wichita Falls and moved Bee there before I left.

Kwang Ju was actually a South Korean Air Force Base. The American Air Force had elements there that could be expanded should the operational need arise. I had been there about two weeks when word was received that our Squadron was to be deactivated. A small communications operating location would remain and I was appointed Commander over twenty-five personnel. Everyone else started shipping out. That summer the Marine squadron from Iwakuni Japan brought their Harrier jets to Kwang Ju for a two-week exercise. The Marines were a great bunch and the exercise went off without a hitch.

In the past, the communications squadron had helped support an orphanage in the city of Kwang Ju. Our small unit continued that support. Life in that orphanage was a harsh bare-bone existence. The children would cling to us like burrs when we visited them. On my first visit I noticed that their toothbrushes were all worn down to the plastic handle. I took new brushes for them the next day. What a difference in how orphans were treated in Korea compared to those I had seen in Norway. My year in Korea slipped on by. My replacement was late in arriving, but I stayed an extra week and left the same day he got to Korea.

I flew back to San Francisco and then on to Dallas where Bee met me at the Airport.

Chapter 26

My new assignment was the Communication Squadron at Kirtland Air Force Base in Albuquerque, New Mexico. We bought a new modest size home and moved in. Judy had re-married. Her new husband, Mike Matherly, had a job offer in Temple, Texas. Judy had graduated from college with a degree as a social worker and she also went to work.

We had been in our new home a week and left on Saturday to go shopping on the Base at Kirtland. We were gone two hours and on our return found the front door had been broken open and we had been robbed. Welcome to Albuquerque! When I went to work on Monday I got another surprise. I learned our Squadron was involved in the clean up of an island in the Pacific, an atomic weapons test site. At our morning briefing the Commander was unhappy with the progress being made. He decided that I should go there. He asked me what I thought. I told him about our break-in at home and that my wife Bee was pretty stressed and I would need to get a twenty-four hour guard if I was going. One of the civilians who worked in Programs volunteered to go, much to my relief.

About a month later the Commander retired and the new Commander, Col. Ludwig, took over. He was an excellent Commander who would eventually become a Two Star General.

My cousin Margaret, with whom I had lived in Scotland, had one daughter named Anne. She married David Harland. He had a photography shop on Guernsey, one of the Channel Islands. David and Anne came to visit us in Albuquerque. David looked and acted sometimes like Inspector Cluseau in the Pink Panther movies. He had no idea how funny he was and I really enjoyed their visit. Their departure ended in a typical Pink Panther scene. I had driven them to the airport in their rental car and was going to return the car for them.

They got out and said their good-byes and went into the airport. Before I could drive off David came rushing out saying he had lost his passport. He thought it might be in the car and proceeded to rip out the seats and back cushions of the car and pile them on the sidewalk, much to the amusement of the people around. Before he could dismantle the car any further, Anne came out of the airport waving his passport that she had found in their luggage. I had hoped they would come for another visit but it has not happened.

Bee had always wanted to get a real estate license so began studying in order to take the test. I spent a lot of time coaching her and when it came time to take the test we both applied and we both passed. I was still in the Air Force and could not do much with my license, but Bee went ahead and started working for one of the local real estate companies. With less than six months to go I approached a small real estate office in our neighborhood to see if I could work part time until I got out of the Air Force. Ray Renard, the owner/broker, agreed and said I could answer the phone and help other agents with open house etc.

One weekend one of the agents asked me to hold an open house on a very nice listing she had, because she wanted to go out of town. I agreed and when Sunday came I put out the open house signs and practiced my sales pitch on the visitors to the property. One young couple wearing blue jeans and driving a motorcycle stopped to look over the place. They did not look like they could afford this home but I gave them the royal welcome and went over all the features of the home, the horse stable and the additional land that could be purchased as an option. They did not appear to be to interested and left after their tour of the property. While at work at the Base on Monday I got an excited call from Ray Renard. He said this same young couple had called the office and wanted me to write up an offer on the property, including the additional acreage. Not only that, they also wanted to list their present home for sale. To make a long story short, I ended up with over six hundred thousand in real estate business.

Chapter 27

After I retired from the Air Force, both Bee and I worked for Ray Renard for about a year. The strip shopping center raised the rent on his office so high that Ray decided to close the office and work out of his home. Bee and I went to work for a company call Hooten-Stahl, the largest real estate company in Albuquerque at that time. Real estate was not as much fun there, but we did make money.

Bee, who had been diagnosed with emphysema, could no longer work after 1986. I worked for two more years and then we started searching for a place to move with a lower altitude than Albuquerque. We sold our rental properties we had accumulated and left Albuquerque.

Since retiring from the United States Air Force in 1978 I have enjoyed an extended retirement and in 2011 have reached the ripe old age of 88, I must have a guardian angel to thank for some close calls. How did only two of us escape that burning plane? How did I find a straw stack in the middle of the only field where they were spreading manure that day?

I loved my years in the United States Air Force, and I am proud to have achieved the rank of Chief Master Sergeant.

In my lifetime I have been blessed with the love of two wonderful women. Bee, who passed away in 1999 and Ruby, whom I married in 2001, continues to make each day a wonder and a delight. Who could ask for more?

Dennis and Ruby Bruno
2001

8290660R0

Made in the USA
Charleston, SC
25 May 2011